CountryLiving

the little book of
Pies & Tarts

★ 50 EASY HOMEMADE FAVORITES TO BAKE & SHARE ★

HEARST BOOKS

A division of Sterling Publishing Co., Inc.

New York / London
www.sterlingpublishing.com

Designer: Anna Christian
Project Editor: Sarah Scheffel

Library of Congress Cataloging-in-Publication Data:
Country living little book of pies & tarts : 50 easy homemade favorites to bake & share.
    p. cm.
  Includes index.
1. Pies. 2. Baking. I. Hearst Books (Firm) II. Country living (New York, N.Y.)
III. Title: Little book of pies & tarts.
  TX773.C637 2011
  641.8′15—dc22

                              2010028936

10 9 8 7 6 5 4 3 2 1

Published by Hearst Books
A Division of Sterling Publishing Co., Inc.
387 Park Avenue South, New York, NY 10016

Country Living is a registered trademark of Hearst Communications, Inc.
www.countryliving.com

For information about custom editions, special sales, premium and corporate purchases, please contact Sterling Special Sales Department at 800-805-5489 or specialsales@sterlingpublishing.com.

Distributed in Canada by Sterling Publishing
c/o Canadian Manda Group, 165 Dufferin Street
Toronto, Ontario, Canada M6K 3H6

Distributed in Australia by Capricorn Link (Australia) Pty. Ltd.
P.O. Box 704, Windsor, NSW 2756 Australia

Manufactured in China

Sterling ISBN 978-1-58816-856-6

contents

easy as pie

Pies and tarts—staples of country cooking—made their way into American hearts long ago. In fact, nothing says "home, sweet home" like the aroma of a freshly baked pie. Rolling and baking a golden-brown piecrust then filling it with ripe seasonal fruit or a delectable savory filling is always a pleasure. But the best part is sharing your homemade creation with friends and family. They will love digging into fresh-from-the-oven slices—plain, à la mode, or topped with a dollop of whipped cream.

Once upon a time, the art of making piecrusts was a basic skill taught to every young woman. Favorite family recipes were coveted, and pie-making tips and techniques were passed down from generation to generation. Unfortunately, many of us today have never been taught this skill, and if we have an archive of favorite family pie recipes, we are not confident in our ability to execute them. That means we rely all too frequently on bakeries to supply us with "homemade" pies for holidays and other special occasions.

The Little Book of Pies & Tarts aims to change that. We teach you the essentials of pie and tart making, then share more than fifty foolproof recipes—along with plenty of tips to help you along the way—so you can make your own pies from scratch with confidence.

We begin with simple crumb crusts. Made from cookie crumbs (and sometimes ground nuts) mixed with butter, sugar, and flavorings, these require little more skill than patting the crumb mixture into a pan. Next come free-form pies like crostatas, which involve rolling out a circle of dough, topping it with a sweet or savory filling, then folding

the edges of the dough around the filling to create a rustic tart. Recipes for easy tarts made from puff pastry (homemade or store-bought) and frozen phyllo dough are also included.

Making free-form pies and tarts prepares you for the challenge of the single-crust and double-crust pies that follow. We provide winning recipes for the classic pies you've always admired but may have considered daunting to bake. Our step-by-step instructions, peppered with tips on technique and enticing full-color photos of the finished creations, make them all easy to tackle. If you want to make apple, blueberry, pumpkin, or strawberry-rhubarb pies, we've got you covered. Or, if you're interested in regional favorites—from key lime to shoofly pie—you'll find the recipes here, along with meringues, mincemeat, and more.

From pies, we move on to elegant tarts and tartlets, always perfect for parties and special occasions. The process is similar to rolling and baking a single-crust pie, but the pastry recipes and pans are unique; see page 108 for details. The book closes with a selection of hand pies and turnovers, individual-serving-sized pies that are easy to make and fun to share.

If you're an experienced pie baker, consider this a refresher course. You are likely to pick up some helpful techniques, along with more than fifty irresistible recipes. If you're new to pie making, this little book is your tutor. Soon you'll be mixing, rolling, and baking beautiful homemade pies and tarts with ease!

BAKING FOR BEGINNERS

If you are a novice baker, here are some tips that will help you feel at home in the kitchen.

ALWAYS READ THE RECIPE THOROUGHLY BEFORE STARTING. Note the oven temperatures, cooking and baking times, and any special equipment you may need. Before you start, gather all the ingredients called for; do not make substitutions unless they are suggested in the recipe.

ACCURATE MEASUREMENTS ARE IMPORTANT IN BAKING. There are two types of measuring cups: those for dry ingredients (like flour and sugar) and those for liquids (such as water and milk). Dry measuring cups are usually made of metal or plastic and come in nested sets that include 1-cup, ½-cup, ⅓-cup, and ¼-cup sizes. Liquid measuring cups are usually made of glass or clear plastic and have a handle and spout for easy pouring; the measurements are marked on the side.

TO MEASURE DRY INGREDIENTS, start by stirring the ingredient in its container, then spoon it into a dry measuring cup. Level off the top with the straightedge of a butter knife, holding the cup over the ingredient container, then transfer the measured amount to your mixing bowl or sifter.

TO MEASURE LIQUIDS PROPERLY, pour the ingredient into a liquid measuring cup, place it on a level surface, and check the measurement at eye level.

BE CAREFUL WHEN WORKING AROUND HOT SURFACES, such as stovetop burners, ovens, and hot pans. Always have an oven mitt at the ready.

PREHEAT YOUR OVEN AS SPECIFIED, and don't be tempted to open the oven door during baking. It's important to maintain even heat during the baking process.

ALLOW YOUR PIE TO COOL AS SPECIFIED IN THE RECIPE. No pie should be served fresh out of the oven—hot fruit filling will burn your tongue! Set hot pie or tart pans on a wire rack to cool so the air can circulate underneath. Depending upon the recipe, the pie may be ready to serve when it has cooled just a bit or when it has reached room

temperature—or you may need to chill it thoroughly. When it's time to serve soft meringue, custard, and cream pies, use a damp serrated knife, wiping the blade between each slice.

IF YOU WANT TO TRANSPORT YOUR PIE to a potluck, picnic, or maybe even a contest at a county fair, baker's boxes (found at restaurant supply stores) are easy and economical. Top the box with one of the recipe-gift cards in the back of the book if your pie is a present! You can also purchase a reusable pie or cake carrier.

THE INGREDIENTS FOR SUCCESS

If you want to become a successful pie baker, you need to start with top-quality ingredients. Here are some tried-and-true tips to help you pick the best.

FRUIT: If strawberries are in season, why bake an apple pie? For the most flavorful (not to mention affordable) pies, choose fruit that is fresh and at its seasonal peak. In the box opposite, we offer tips on selecting, sweetening, and peeling pie-perfect fruit. Don't have any fresh fruit on hand? If you have your heart set on a fruit pie, select a good-quality canned or frozen fruit that does not contain excessive amounts of sugar.

BUTTER: Butter is the key to sweet and delectable crusts, but some excellent recipes also include vegetable shortening for a flakier texture. Choose a brand of butter that you have come to trust, and be sure to check the sell-by dates to ensure freshness. It is critical that your butter be well chilled before you begin making the dough. Otherwise, you'll end up with an unwieldy crust that's difficult to work

with and has an inferior texture after baking.

For the best results, freeze the butter pieces for a short while (20 to 30 minutes) before you begin, then chop it into small pieces. If you have cool hands, rub the butter into the flour with your fingertips; if your hands are hot, it's best to use a pastry blender or two knives. After mixing, allow the dough to rest for at least 30 minutes to give the gluten time to relax. This makes the dough less elastic and easier to roll.

< **12** >

FLOUR: Most of the recipes in this book call for all-purpose flour. Choose a premium brand and store it at cool room temperature in a tightly sealed canister, tin, or plastic container to keep it fresh. Whole-wheat flour is best stored in the freezer; if it's kept at room temperature, it can become rancid. The recipes in the book usually call for all-purpose flour. If you want to make your crust a little more tender, you can use all-purpose flour mixed with an equal weight of cake or pastry flour, a fine-textured, soft-wheat flour with a high starch content. Sift flour if the recipe directs it.

SUGAR: You'll need granulated, brown, and confectioners' sugar to make the recipes in this book. Store these in tightly sealed containers to keep out humidity, which will cause them to clump.

Fruit Know-How

Whether you pick it yourself or purchase it from a farmer's market or grocery, here's how to get the most from your fruit.

Go for ripe: Mature fruit at the height of the season is always the most flavorful. Smell, taste, and feel are all good indicators of ripeness.

Sweeten with sugar: Some harvests will yield sweeter fruits than others, so taste to assess how much sugar you need to add. Sugar can do wonders to bring out the flavor in even slightly underripe fruits.

Don't automatically peel: The most intense flavor in a fruit is found in the peel, so if it is not tough, consider leaving the peel on when using fruits like peaches and plums.

Use your freezer: To enjoy summer berries year-round, wash ripe berries in a colander then set on paper towels to dry. Spread them in a single layer on baking sheets and freeze for 2 hours before transferring them to heavy-duty freezer bags. (Expel air from bags before freezing.)

TOOLS OF THE TRADE

You don't need an arsenal of fancy tools to bake a pie, but here are some basics you'll want to have on hand. Many are things you probably already have in your kitchen; some, as noted, you can do without.

BOWLS: A set of nesting bowls in graduated sizes from 1 to 3 quarts will see you through most pie-baking endeavors (or baking endeavors of any kind). Plastic bowls absorb fat, which is a problem when you need a grease-free bowl (for beating egg whites, for instance). Heat-proof glass, ceramic, and stainless-steel bowls are all better choices. To keep a bowl from skating around the counter as you mix, place a damp kitchen towel or paper towels under it.

DRY AND LIQUID MEASURING CUPS: See our overview on page 9. You will also need a set of measuring spoons, which can be used for both dry and liquid ingredients.

WOODEN SPOONS AND A RUBBER SPATULA: Wooden spoons are gentle on dough and won't burn your fingers if you use them to stir hot pie fillings. Choose spoons made of hardwoods like maple; they should be smoothly finished and free of rough patches that might splinter off. You will also want a rubber spatula for scraping dough off the side of the bowl and getting every last drop of filling into the pie.

PASTRY BLENDER: If you find it difficult to cut butter or shortening into the flour mixture using two knives (and your hands are too hot!), try a pastry blender. Its straight handle is fitted with a curved sweep of tines or wires that make mixing pie dough easy. Look out for vintage versions at tag sales and flea markets.

ROLLING PIN: We recommend the kind with handles and a free-spinning roller. Choose a heavy rolling pin (at least 4 pounds); the weight itself will do most of the work, so you'll never have to lean into it. In a pinch, a wine bottle is a decent substitute for a rolling pin.

PIE PANS OR TINS: Made of ovenproof glass, ceramic, or metal, pie plates come in 8-, 9-, and 10-inch sizes. Crusts brown best in glass pans. Disposable pie pans are useful if you're baking a pie for a gift, but check the size—they often have a smaller capacity than durable pans.

TART PANS: These come in a wide range of sizes and shapes, from tiny 2-inch tartlets to huge 13-inch rounds. They can be square or rectangular, as well as circular. Many also come with

removable bottoms, which is handy if you want to unmold your tart without risk of damage to the lovely golden-brown crust. (See page 108 for more details.) If you want to stick with just one tart pan, get a simple 9-inch round one. It will allow you to prepare the majority of the tart recipes in this book.

PIE WEIGHTS: A piecrust baked blind (without the filling in it) needs to be weighted in the center to keep it from bubbling and buckling. Many bakers use dried beans for this purpose (and reuse them again and again). You can also purchase packets of small, bean-shaped aluminum pie weights. Line the bottom of the crust with aluminum foil or parchment before placing the weights on top.

COOLING RACKS: Pies and tarts should be cooled on a wire rack to allow the air to circulate.

FOOD PROCESSOR: While certainly not necessary, a food processor makes mixing pie dough a breeze. Several recipes in this book provide instructions for doing just that. You'll need a metal blade attachment.

ESSENTIAL TECHNIQUES

Making a pie (or tart) crust is easier than you think. Here we walk you through the process, step by step. Instructions will vary slightly from recipe to recipe, however, so be sure to read through your chosen recipe before you begin.

MIX THE DOUGH: With a pastry blender (or two knives used scissor-fashion), "chop" the butter or shortening into the dry ingredients until crumb-like.

FLATTEN IT INTO A ROUND: Before rolling, let chilled dough stand at room temperature 5 minutes. With a floured rolling pin on a floured surface, flatten the dough into a round.

ROLL IT OUT: Roll out the dough to the size and thickness specified in the recipe (usually a couple inches larger than the pan size). Give the round an occasional quarter-turn as you roll; if it sticks, sprinkle the surface with a little flour.

TRANSFER TO PAN: Fold half of the dough round over the rolling pin. Center the rolling pin over the pie or tart pan and let the dough roll off the pin onto the pan. Pat the pie with your fingers so it conforms to the shape of the pan. To finish single-crust pies with decorative edges, see page 56 to 57. To shape a tart crust and finish the edges, see instructions on page 108.

BLIND BAKE: Recipes often instruct you to prebake (or "blind" bake) the crust before you add the filling. First prick the bottom of the crust all over with a fork. This will help keep the crust from blistering as it bakes.

LINE WITH WEIGHTS: Next, line it with foil and fill it with dry beans, metal pie weights, or uncooked rice. This will prevent the crust from puffing up and shrinking as it bakes. Then blind bake the crust for the time indicated in the recipe. If you are making a single-crust pie or a tart, cool the prebaked shell, then fill it and bake for the time indicated in the recipe. If it's a double-crust pie, see Add the Top Crust, next.

NOW ADD THE TOP CRUST: If you are making a double-crust pie, cool the prebaked pie shell, then add the sweet or savory filling. Roll out the top crust and position on top of the pie, leaving a 1-inch overhang. Fold the edges under and seal them, then create a decorative edge, if you like (see pages 56 to 57 for options, from a simple pattern made with the tines of a fork to a fancy border decorated with tiny hearts or leaves). Cut several 1-inch slits in the top of the pie to let steam escape, or create a decorative window (see page 82 for photo and directions). Then bake your pie for the time indicated in the recipe.

SHAPE A TART CRUST: With a fluted tart pan, you don't have to worry about finishing the edges like you do for pies. Just press the dough gently into the rim so that it fills all the indentations. Let the dough hang loosely over the edge of the pan.

TRIM A TART CRUST: To trim off the excess dough, simply roll a rolling pin over the edges of the pan; the rim will act as a cutting edge and the dough will fall away as shown here. Now you can blind bake your crust (see instructions opposite) or simply add the filling and bake it.

Pie Baker's Cheat Sheet

► MAKING ◄

If you're an experienced baker, you most likely have your own ideas about how to make a winning piecrust. But if you're new to the game, these pointers will help you turn out crusts you'll be proud to call your own. Throughout the book, we provide additional tips to help you with every step of the pie- and tart-making process.

Flakiness: Butter tastes better but melts faster than shortening. Use a tablespoon or two of shortening in place of the equal amount of butter to achieve a flakier crust. Also, be sure to keep your ingredients cold. If you have time, freeze them for about 20 minutes before you begin.

Fit: Lightly dusted parchment paper is the perfect rolling surface. If there's a chance your dough will get warm while you're rolling it, use parchment so you can easily transfer it to the refrigerator to rechill. To fit the rolled-out circle of dough into the pie pan, center the rolling pin over the pie pan, then let the dough roll off the rolling pin onto the pan.

► BAKING ◄

There's more to baking a pie than just popping it in the oven. Several different factors need to be considered. Follow this advice to help it emerge from the oven looking gorgeous.

Prebake: If your piecrust will be filled with a supermoist filling, such as blueberries, the crust should be baked slightly before filling to prevent it from getting soggy at the bottom. See page 15 for tips on weighting the crust before you prebake.

Bake: Don't ruin a crust rim by burning it before the filling is cooked. Fit strips of aluminum foil around the pie edge to prevent overbrowning.

The finish: If a pie is almost done baking but it hasn't yet turned golden, mix an egg yolk with 1 tablespoon cream and lightly brush it over the crust. For a touch of sparkle, sprinkle it with granulated sugar (this can also be done before you start baking). Or use sanding sugar, found at baking supply stores; it provides more glitter.

simple crumb crusts

LET THEM EAT CRUMBS!

If you're a pie-baking novice (or just really busy!), crumb crusts are your ally. They are the easiest of all crusts to make—simply combine cookie crumbs of choice with melted butter and flavorings, pat the mixture into a pan, and bake. Crumb crusts can be dressed up with coconut flakes, nuts, vanilla, or spices, and they stand up well against moist fillings such as creams, puddings, and meringues.

PREPARING THE PAN AND SHAPING THE CRUST: You don't need to grease the pan. There should be enough butter in the crust to keep it from sticking. Using your fingers, pat the crumb mixture evenly onto the bottom of the pan, then press it up the side of the pan.

How Many Cookies Do You Need?

Generally you need 1½ cups cookie crumbs to make a 9-inch piecrust. That's about . . .

- ▶ **10** graham crackers (the full rectangles)
- ▶ **30** gingersnaps (2-inch size)
- ▶ **45** vanilla wafers (1½-inch size)
- ▶ **27** chocolate wafers (2½-inch size)

But follow the quantities specified in individual recipes.

BAKED VERSUS UN-BAKED CRUSTS: Typically, baking a crumb crust blends the flavors and also makes it firmer, crisper, and more resistant to becoming soggy. If you plan to add a cold filling that doesn't need to be baked, such as pudding, prebake your crust. If the filling does need to bake, prebaking the crust is not necessary. Follow the directions specified in the individual recipe.

PREBAKING OR BAKING A CRUMB CRUST: Chill the crust for at least 30 minutes so it won't slide down the side of the pan. Preheat the oven to the temperature specified in the recipe. Prebake the crust for the required time or until it puffs and colors slightly, then cool it completely and refrigerate it for at least 30 minutes before adding the filling. If the filling needs to be baked, add it to the chilled crust just before baking and cool completely before serving.

Crumb Crust Three Ways

This basic cookie-crumb crust can be made with graham crackers, gingersnaps, or vanilla wafers. Choose your favorite cookie or select the best flavor match for your intended filling. We use the vanilla-wafer version for our Banana Pudding Pie on page 26.

MAKES: ONE 9-INCH PIECRUST (8 SERVINGS)

1½ cups fine cookie crumbs, such as graham cracker, gingersnap, or vanilla wafer (see equivalents, opposite)

2 tablespoons sugar

5 tablespoons butter or margarine, melted

1. Preheat the oven to 375°F. In a medium-size bowl, with a fork, stir crumbs and sugar with melted butter until evenly blended and moistened. With your hand, press the mixture onto the bottom and up the side of a 9-inch pie pan or 9-inch tart pan with removable bottom.

2. Bake the crust 8 to 10 minutes. Cool completely on a wire rack.

NUTRITION PER ¹/₁₀ **GRAHAM-CRACKER CRUST: calories: 120; 1 g protein; 13 g carbohydrate; 7 g fat; 1 g fiber; 160 mg sodium; 0 mg cholesterol**

NUTRITION PER ¹/₁₀ **GINGERSNAP CRUST: calories: 145; 1 g protein; 19 g carbohydrate; 8 g fat; 1 g fiber; 215 mg sodium; 0 mg cholesterol**

NUTRITION PER ¹/₁₀ **VANILLA-WAFER CRUST: calories: 190; 1 g protein; 22 g carbohydrate; 11 g fat; 1 g fiber; 160 mg sodium; 0 mg cholesterol**

Banana Pudding Pie

A retro dessert is turned into an irresistible pie
featuring fresh bananas, a crust made from
vanilla wafers, and loads of gooey caramel.

MAKES: ONE 9-INCH PIE (10 SERVINGS)

1 recipe prebaked Vanilla-Wafer Crumb Crust (page 25)

3 egg yolks

2 tablespoons cornstarch

1/2 cup granulated sugar

1/4 teaspoon salt

1 teaspoon powdered gelatin

1 cup whole milk, chilled

1 cup heavy cream

1 vanilla bean, pod and scraped seeds

1 1/2 teaspoons unsalted butter

3/4 teaspoon pure vanilla extract

1 cup fresh whipped cream

5 tablespoons caramel sauce, store-bought or homemade (page 37), plus extra for garnish

3 medium bananas, sliced

1. Place a medium-size bowl in a larger bowl filled with ice water and set aside. In another bowl, whisk the egg yolks, cornstarch, sugar, and salt together until very thick and light in color. Set aside. Sprinkle gelatin over 1/4 cup of the cold milk. Let sit for 5 minutes.

2. Bring the cream, remaining 3/4 cup milk, and vanilla bean and seeds to a boil in a medium pot. Slowly whisk the warm cream mixture into the egg mixture, pour the custard back into the pot, and cook, stirring, over medium-low heat until it reaches a boil. Pour the custard through a fine-mesh strainer into the prepared chilled bowl, stir in the gelatin mixture, butter, and vanilla extract. Let cool and fold in whipped cream to create the pudding.

3. Spread caramel sauce over the prepared crust, reserving 1 tablespoon to drizzle on top of pie. Line the crust with slices from 2 1/2 bananas and top them with the pudding. Chill for 2 hours. Decorate the pie with the remaining banana slices and caramel.

NUTRITION PER SERVING: calories: 470; protein: 4 g; fat: 28 g; carbohydrate: 56 g; fiber: 2 g; sodium: 184 mg; cholesterol: 115 mg

Yogurt and Fruit Tartlets with Cereal Crusts

A quick, fresh, and healthful treat. The crisp tart shells are made with crushed cereal, almonds, and maple syrup and require just ten minutes to bake. Yogurt makes a creamy high-calcium filling. Top with your choice of berries or sliced fruit. You will need eight 4-inch fluted tart pans with removable bottoms.

MAKES: 8 TARTLETS

5 cups cornflakes

1 cup pecan halves

4 tablespoons (½ stick) unsalted butter, melted

6 tablespoons maple syrup

1 (16-ounce) container plain yogurt

1 (16-ounce) container vanilla yogurt

2⅔ cups fresh fruit (such as grapes, blueberries, and raspberries)

1. Preheat the oven to 350°F. Place eight 4-inch round tart pans with removable bottoms on a baking sheet; set aside. In the bowl of a food processor fitted with a metal blade, process the cornflakes and pecans until combined—about 10 short pulses. Transfer the crumb mixture to a large bowl, drizzle it with the melted butter, and toss to combine. Stir in the maple syrup. Evenly divide the cereal mixture among the tart pans and press it into the bottoms and sides to form shells. Bake for 10 minutes. Transfer to a wire rack to cool completely.

2. Remove each shell from its mold and transfer it to a serving plate. Mix the yogurts together and top each tart shell with ¼ cup yogurt and ⅓ cup fruit. Serve immediately.

NUTRITION PER SERVING: calories: 350; protein: 8 g; fat: 19 g; carbohydrate: 40 g; fiber: 2g; sodium: 245 mg; cholesterol: 28 mg

Rhubarb Custard Pie with Pecan Crust

Celebrate the first spring rhubarb with this simple, luscious pie. The nutty crust contrasts nicely with the creamy filling.

MAKES: ONE 9-INCH PIE (8 SERVINGS)

CRUST

½ cup pecan halves

1⅓ cups all-purpose flour

½ cup sugar

½ cup (1 stick) unsalted butter, chilled and cut into pieces

2 large egg yolks

1 tablespoon pure vanilla extract

1 large egg white

1 teaspoon water

FILLING

1¼ pounds rhubarb, trimmed and coarsely chopped (4 cups)

⅔ cup sugar

1 teaspoon grated lemon zest

¼ teaspoon salt

2 large eggs

1 large egg yolk

1¼ cups heavy cream

1 tablespoon cornstarch

1. **Make the crust:** Preheat the oven to 400°F. In a food processor fitted with a metal blade, process the pecans until finely ground. Add the flour and sugar; process until combined. Add the butter, egg yolks, and vanilla; process until the mixture resembles coarse crumbs.

2. Press the crumb mixture into the bottom and up the sides of a 9-inch pie pan; crimp decoratively along the edge. With the tines of a fork, prick the bottom and sides of the crust. In a small bowl, mix together the egg white and water. Brush the bottom and sides of the crust with the egg wash. Bake until golden brown—10 to 12 minutes. Transfer to a wire rack to cool completely. Reduce the oven temperature to 350°F.

3. **Make the filling:** In a large bowl, combine the rhubarb, sugar, lemon zest, and salt. Spoon the filling into the crust. In a medium-size bowl, beat together the eggs and egg yolk. Mix in the cream and cornstarch. Spoon over the rhubarb mixture.

4. **Finish the pie:** Cover the edge of the crust with foil to prevent overbrowning, then bake the pie until the custard is firm—25 to 30 minutes. Transfer to a wire rack to cool completely.

NUTRITION PER SERVING: calories: 525; protein: 7 g; fat: 33 g; carbohydrate: 51 g; fiber: 3g; sodium: 207 mg; cholesterol: 212 mg

Summer Berry Tart with Chocolate-Crumb Crust

This dessert looks oh so impressive, but it is not difficult to make.
You start with a chocolate wafer crust, layer on a custard
scented with vanilla and orange zest, and top it all with
fresh berries and a currant jelly glaze. For a flavor alternative,
substitute shortbread cookies for the chocolate wafers
and use your favorite berries and jelly.

MAKES: ONE 9-INCH SQUARE TART (9 SERVINGS)

6 tablespoons unsalted butter

2 cups finely crushed chocolate wafer cookies

5 tablespoons honey

2 cups whole milk

1 vanilla bean, pod and scraped seeds

3 (1/2-inch-wide) strips orange zest

5 large egg yolks

3 tablespoons sugar

2 tablespoons all-purpose flour

2 tablespoons cornstarch

1/4 cup fresh whipped cream

3/4 cup red currants

2 1/2 cups blueberries

3/4 cup currant jelly

1 tablespoon water

1. Preheat the oven to 350°F. Melt 5 tablespoons butter and toss with the crushed cookies and 1 tablespoon honey. Press the mixture into a 9-inch square tart pan. Bake until firm—12 to 15 minutes. Cool completely.

2. Fill a large bowl halfway with ice water and place a slightly smaller bowl on top; set aside. Heat the milk, vanilla bean and seeds, and orange zest in a large saucepan over medium heat just to a boil. Remove the pan from the heat and let steep for 20 minutes. Whisk the egg yolks, remaining 1/4 cup honey, and sugar in a large bowl until thick and pale yellow. Sift the flour and cornstarch over the egg mixture and whisk until smooth. Reheat the milk to just boiling, and whisk a few tablespoons at a time into the egg mixture. Transfer the custard back to the saucepan and cook, whisking constantly, over medium heat until the mixture begins to bubble and thickens—about 3 minutes longer. Strain the custard into the bowl in the ice bath. Dot the custard with the remaining 1 tablespoon butter. Cover with plastic wrap placed directly on the surface and cool completely.

3. Fold the whipped cream into the custard. Spread it into the cookie shell and top it with the currants and berries. Heat the jelly and water. Dab the glaze over the fruit. Chill for about 30 minutes.

NUTRITION PER SERVING: calories: 670; protein: 6 g; fat: 17 g; carbohydrate: 129 g; fiber: 3 g; sodium: 234 mg; cholesterol: 148 mg

Pumpkin Cream Tartlets with Gingersnap Crust

With our easy gingersnap cookie crust, there's no fuss or muss.
You simply mix the cookie crumbs and butter in a bowl,
then pat the mixture into tartlet pans. Finish with the sweet-tart
cranberry topping for a holiday-worthy presentation.

MAKES: 8 TARTLETS

CRUST

**3 cups gingersnap crumbs
(about 50 cookies)**

2 teaspoons ground cinnamon

**3/4 cup (1 1/2 sticks) unsalted
butter, melted**

CRANBERRY TOPPING

2 cups sugar

1/2 cup water

1 cup fresh cranberries

PUMPKIN CREAM FILLING

1/2 cup whole milk

1 teaspoon unflavored gelatin

1 cup pureed pumpkin

3/4 cup sugar

2 tablespoons brandy or cognac

4 teaspoons ground cinnamon

1/4 teaspoon ground nutmeg

1/4 teaspoon ground cloves

4 large egg yolks

**1 cup heavy cream, whipped
to stiff peaks**

1. **Make the crusts:** Preheat the oven to 350°F. In a large bowl, combine the crumbs, cinnamon, and butter. Press the crumb mixture into the bottom and up the sides of eight 3½-inch tartlet pans with removable bottoms. Place the tartlet shells on a baking sheet and bake for 10 minutes. Transfer them to a wire rack to cool completely.

2. **Make the cranberry topping:** In a small saucepan, bring the sugar and water to a boil over high heat. Add the cranberries and cook until they just begin to soften. With a slotted spoon, transfer the cranberries to a small bowl and set them aside. Reserve the cranberry syrup for another use.

3. **Make the filling:** Fill a large bowl with ice and water and set aside. Place the milk in a small bowl, sprinkle the gelatin over it, and set aside. In a large saucepan, combine the pumpkin puree, sugar, brandy, cinnamon, nutmeg, cloves, and egg yolks. Cook the pumpkin mixture over medium heat, whisking constantly, until it begins to bubble and the temperature registers 140°F on an instant-read thermometer. Stir in the milk mixture and cook 1 minute more; transfer the custard to a medium-size bowl and set it over the prepared ice bath, stirring occasionally, until cool—about 10 minutes. Fold the whipped cream into the chilled pumpkin custard.

4. Divide the filling among the cooled crusts and smooth the tops. Chill for 6 hours or overnight.

5. Top each tartlet with a spoonful of candied cranberries, and serve cold.

NUTRITION PER SERVING: calories: 430; protein: 5 g; fat: 25 g; carbohydrate: 46 g; fiber: 3g; sodium: 177 mg; cholesterol: 173 mg

Chocolate-Caramel Cream Pie

Chocoholics will adore this rich pie, which boasts a chocolate filling and a chocolate wafer crust. Top with our homemade caramel sauce or use your favorite store-bought brand. For photo, see page 22.

MAKES: ONE 9-INCH PIE (12 SERVINGS)

½ **cup (1 stick) unsalted butter**

2 cups (about 36 cookies) finely crushed chocolate wafer cookies

2 tablespoons cognac

5 ounces bittersweet chocolate, finely chopped

4 large egg yolks

⅔ **cup plus 2 tablespoons dark brown sugar**

1 tablespoon cornstarch

⅛ **teaspoon salt**

2 cups plus 2 tablespoons heavy cream

1 cup plus 2 tablespoons whole milk

1½ **teaspoons pure vanilla extract**

1 recipe Caramel Sauce (recipe follows)

1 tablespoon cocoa powder

1. Preheat the oven to 350°F. Melt 4 tablespoons butter and combine it with the cookie crumbs and cognac in a medium-size bowl. Press the crumb mixture into the bottom and up the sides of a 9-inch pie pan. Bake for 10 minutes, then cool completely on a wire rack.

2. Place the chocolate in a large bowl and set aside. Whisk the egg yolks, ⅔ cup brown sugar, cornstarch, and salt in a medium-size bowl and set aside. Heat ½ cup plus 2 tablespoons of the cream, the milk, and the remaining 4 tablespoons butter in a medium-size saucepan over medium-high heat until the mixture just begins to boil. Whisking continuously, gradually pour the hot milk in to the egg mixture. Return the custard to the saucepan and, whisking continuously, cook it over medium heat until it comes to a boil. Cook for 1 more minute, still whisking, and stir in 1 teaspoon vanilla. Strain the pudding into the bowl with the chocolate. Let sit for 2 minutes to allow the chocolate to melt, then use a rubber spatula to fold the mixture together. Cool to room temperature.

3. Pour the caramel sauce into the piecrust and refrigerate for 10 minutes. Spread the pudding over the caramel and chill for 2 hours. Beat the remaining $1\frac{1}{2}$ cups cream, 2 tablespoons brown sugar, and $\frac{1}{2}$ teaspoon vanilla, and the cocoa powder in a large bowl until stiff peaks form. Spread over the pudding and chill for 30 minutes or up to 6 hours before serving.

★ ★ ★

Caramel Sauce

This caramel sauce is so good, you'll be licking your spoon.
Just take care not to burn your tongue!

$\frac{3}{4}$ **cup sugar**

$\frac{1}{4}$ **cup water**

$\frac{1}{4}$ **cup heavy cream**

1 tablespoon unsalted butter

Combine the sugar and water in a small saucepan over medium heat, stirring occasionally until the sugar dissolves. Increase the temperature to high and cook until the caramel turns an amber color. Remove the pan from the heat and stir in the cream, $\frac{1}{8}$ cup at a time, until smooth. Add the butter and stir until melted. Cool until the sauce has thickened slightly, then use immediately or refrigerate in a microwaveable container for up to 3 weeks. To reheat, microwave on high for 1 to 2 minutes, stirring twice.

NUTRITION PER SERVING OF PIE: calories: 400; protein: 4 g; fat: 32 g; carbohydrate: 26 g; fiber: 1 g; sodium: 119 mg; cholesterol: 132 mg

no-fuss free-form crusts

CROSTATAS, GALETTES, AND OTHER CASUAL CRUSTS

If preparing a pie or tart crust seems daunting (or you're short on time), try the no-fuss alternatives in this chapter. These free-form crusts are as delicious and attractive as any pie, but they are virtually foolproof to make. No need to concern yourself about kitchen temperature, lengthy chilling times, or blind baking the dough. You can forget about pie tins and tart pans, too. All you need is a rolling pin and parchment paper, a bowl, and a baking sheet.

Whether you call it a crostata, like the Italians, or a galette, like the French, you can make and serve this style of hand-shaped tart within an hour. The rich puff pastry dough mixes easily; just roll it flat, mound the filling in the center (sweet and fruity or savory, your choice), then fold the edges quickly up and over to create your tart. You can also buy easy-to-use pre-made puff pastry sheets in the freezer section of your supermarket.

Perfect Pastries

▶ Use a heavy-duty baking sheet to ensure that the tart's crust does not overcook before the filling is ready.

▶ Our tarts serve 4 to 8, but these recipes are easy to double, so why not make two tarts? To reheat, bring to room temperature and warm in a preheated 325°F oven.

▶ Once you master the basics, you can vary your fillings. Go with peaches, cherries, apricots, or whatever fruit is seasonal. A sprinkling of flour and sugar absorbs the fruits' sweet juices.

▶ To give the crust a pretty finish, glaze the edges with an egg wash (or use heavy cream) and sprinkle on a liberal helping of sugar.

Shaping a tart from phyllo is another easy way to go. A Middle Eastern specialty, phyllo consists of paper-thin sheets of dough used to make flaky pies and pastries like honey-steeped baklava. This, too, is available in the freezer case of most grocery stores; simply unroll the sheets, layer them (brushing them with butter or oil as you go), and cut them to the desired size.

Quick Puff Pastry

Here is a simple version of this French classic.
It is used in the Caramelized-Onion and
Gruyère Tarts on page 50.

MAKES: ABOUT 1 ³/₄ POUNDS

2 ¹/₂ cups all-purpose flour, chilled

1 teaspoon salt

1 ¹/₂ cups (3 sticks) unsalted butter, frozen for 1 hour

³/₄ cup ice water

1. Fit a food processor with the largest of the grater attachments or freeze a metal box grater with large holes. Combine the flour and salt and set aside. Quickly grate the butter and add it to the flour mixture. Rechill the butter and flour if necessary. Add the ice water to the bowl and stir until just combined—the dough will be a loose, shaggy mass.

2. Transfer the dough to a well-floured surface and roll and shape it into a long rectangle about 6 by 18 inches. Using a large spatula, fold or flip the bottom portion of the dough toward the middle and bring the top part of the dough downward to the edge, as if you were folding a business letter. Rotate the dough a quarter turn to the right so that the shorter end of the dough is closer to you and again roll it out into a 6-by-18-inch rectangle.

3. Repeat the folding and turning, then roll out the dough and fold it once more. Wrap the dough in plastic wrap and refrigerate it for at least 30 minutes or up to 24 hours. The dough can also be wrapped in plastic and frozen for up to 2 months.

NUTRITION PER SERVING: calories: 510; protein: 5 g; fat: 40 g; carbohydrate: 34 g; fiber: 2 g; sodium: 311 mg; cholesterol: 106 mg

Rustic Apple-Pomegranate Tart

A pomegranate glaze dresses up this rustic apple tart.
Cinnamon scents the dough.

MAKES: ONE 12-INCH TART (8 SERVINGS)

CINNAMON PASTRY

1 1/2 cups unsifted all-purpose flour

2 teaspoons sugar

1 teaspoon ground cinnamon

1/4 teaspoon salt

1/2 cup (1 stick) unsalted butter, chilled

1 large egg

3 tablespoons ice water

FILLING

2 tablespoons unsalted butter

3 large Granny Smith apples, peeled, cored, and sliced 1/8 inch thick

3 large Golden Delicious apples, peeled, cored, and sliced 1/8 inch thick

1/4 cup sugar

1/8 teaspoon salt

GLAZE

1 large pomegranate

1/4 cup sugar

1 tablespoon fresh lemon juice

1. **Prepare the cinnamon pastry:** In a medium-size bowl, combine the flour, sugar, cinnamon, and salt. Cut in the butter with a pastry blender, 2 knives, or your fingers until the mixture resembles very coarse crumbs. In a cup, use a fork to beat the egg and ice water until well combined. Measure 1 tablespoon egg mixture into another cup and set aside. Add the remaining egg mixture to the flour mixture, tossing lightly with a fork until the pastry is moist enough to hold together. Wrap and set the pastry aside at room temperature until you are ready to assemble the tart.

2. **Prepare the filling:** In a large heavy skillet, melt the butter. Add the apples and cook, stirring constantly, until they are just tender and most of the liquid has evaporated. Stir in the sugar and salt; set aside to cool slightly.

3. Preheat the oven to 375°F. Between 1 sheet of parchment paper or heavy-duty aluminum foil and 1 sheet of waxed paper, roll out the floured pastry to a 15-inch round. Remove the waxed paper; place the pastry, still on the parchment, on a rimmed baking sheet.

4. Transfer the filling to the center of the pastry, leaving a 3-inch border. Fold the edges of the pastry over the filling. Brush the pastry with the reserved egg mixture. Bake for 35 minutes, or until brown and bubbling. Transfer the tart, on the parchment, to a wire rack to cool completely.

5. **While the tart bakes, prepare the glaze:** Quarter the pomegranate and remove the seeds from the membrane; discard the shell and membrane. Set aside 3 tablespoons of the seeds. Place the remaining seeds in a blender and liquefy. Pour the pomegranate juice through a strainer into a 1-quart saucepan. Add the sugar and lemon juice and heat to boiling. Cook for 5 minutes or until thickened. Sprinkle the reserved seeds over the apple filling in the still-warm tart and drizzle glaze over all. Let cool to room temperature.

NUTRITION PER SERVING: calories: 295; protein: 4 g; fat: 10 g; carbohydrate: 50 g; fiber: 3 g; sodium: 198 mg; cholesterol: 50 mg

Mixed Berry Crostata

This free-form tart is simple to make and very adaptable.
You can substitute equal amounts of peaches, plums, or apricots
for the berries or use half berries and half stone fruits.

MAKES: ONE 8-INCH CROSTATA (6 SERVINGS)

1¼ cups plus 1 tablespoon all-purpose flour

¼ cup plus 2 tablespoons granulated sugar

⅛ teaspoon salt

½ cup (1 stick) unsalted butter, softened

2 large eggs

1 cup fresh raspberries

1 cup fresh blackberries

1 tablespoon fresh lemon juice

1 tablespoon turbinado sugar (optional)

1. **Make the pastry:** Combine 1¼ cups flour, ¼ cup granulated sugar, and salt in a large bowl. Lightly beat one of the eggs. Form a well in the center of the dry ingredients and place the butter and the beaten egg in the well. Using your hands, mix the ingredients into a soft, pliable dough. Form it into a 4-inch disk and place it on a lightly floured sheet of parchment paper. Lightly dust the dough with flour and roll it into a 10-inch circle. Place the dough, still on the parchment, on a baking sheet, cover it with plastic wrap, and chill for 10 minutes. Preheat the oven to 375°F and position the rack in the middle.

2. **Assemble the crostata:** In a small bowl, mix the remaining flour and granulated sugar and set aside. Evenly sprinkle the flour-and-sugar mixture on the dough, leaving a 1-inch-wide border around the edge. Place berries on top of the mixture and sprinkle with the lemon juice. Fold the border over the top of the berries to form an 8-inch tart.

3. **Bake the crostata:** Beat the remaining egg and lightly brush the top of the dough border with the mixture; sprinkle it with turbinado sugar, if desired. Bake for about 35 minutes. Slide the crostata, on the parchment paper, onto a wire rack and let it cool for 1 hour. Serve warm or at room temperature.

NUTRITION PER SERVING: calories: 340; protein: 5 g; fat: 18 g; carbohydrate: 41 g; fiber: 3 g; sodium: 68 mg; cholesterol: 112 mg

Plum Galette

This easy-to-form pastry is filled with ripe plums and toasted almonds. The dough can be made up to three days ahead, and you can bake the galette up to three hours before serving.

MAKES: ONE 8-INCH GALETTE (8 SERVINGS)

PASTRY

1½ cups unsifted all-purpose flour

1 tablespoon granulated sugar

½ teaspoon salt

6 tablespoons unsalted butter, chilled and cut into pieces

3 tablespoons vegetable shortening, chilled

5 to 6 tablespoons ice water

FILLING

2 pounds (6 to 7) ripe sweet plums, each pitted and sliced into 8 pieces

½ cup granulated sugar

¼ cup sliced almonds, toasted

3 tablespoons all-purpose flour

1 tablespoon fresh lemon juice

¼ teaspoon ground nutmeg

2 tablespoons heavy cream

1 tablespoon coarse brown sugar

Crème fraîche or sweetened whipped cream (optional)

1. **Prepare the pastry:** In the bowl of a food processor fitted with the chopping blade, combine the flour, granulated sugar, and salt; pulse to mix. Add the butter and shortening and pulse at 5-second intervals, just until the texture resembles coarse crumbs. Add the ice water, 1 tablespoon at a time, and process until a loose ball forms. Flatten the pastry into a disk. Wrap and refrigerate the dough for at least 30 minutes or up to 3 days.

2. **Prepare the filling:** Preheat the oven to 400°F. In a large bowl, combine the plums, granulated sugar, almonds, flour, lemon juice, and nutmeg. Toss and set aside.

3. Between 2 sheets of waxed paper, roll out the floured pastry to a 14-inch round or oval. Remove 1 sheet of waxed paper and invert the pastry onto a baking pan; peel off the remaining sheet of waxed paper.

4. Spoon filling into center of the pastry, leaving a 3-inch border. Lift the edges of pastry and fold them up and over the filling. Brush the pastry with the cream and sprinkle with the brown sugar.

5. Bake the tart for 25 minutes, then cover it with aluminum foil. Bake until the filling bubbles and pastry has lightly browned—15 to 20 minutes more. Transfer the baking pan to a wire rack to cool completely. To serve, top each slice of the galette with a dollop of crème fraîche, if desired.

NUTRITION PER SERVING: calories: 370; protein: 4 g; fat: 17 g; carbohydrate: 51 g; fiber: 3 g; sodium: 210 mg; cholesterol: 28 mg

Prosciutto and Fig Crostata

Prosciutto and figs is a classic Italian combination, so why not use them as crostata toppers? The saltiness of the prosciutto is beautifully balanced by the deep sweetness of the figs.

MAKES: ONE 12-INCH CROSTATA (6 SERVINGS)

4 ounces dried Black Mission figs

1/4 cup fresh lemon juice

1 tablespoon fresh thyme leaves

2 cloves garlic

1/2 teaspoon coarse sea salt

1 (9-inch) store-bought unroll-and-fill piecrust, or 1/4 recipe Grandma's Pie Dough (page 85)

4 ounces (1/2 package) cream cheese, softened

2 ounces prosciutto, cut into 1/2-inch-wide strips

1 large egg white

1. Preheat the oven to 425°F. Place the figs, lemon juice, thyme, garlic, and salt in the bowl of a food processor fitted with a metal blade and process to a smooth paste. Set aside.

2. Roll the dough into a 13-inch circle on a lightly floured surface. Transfer the round to a baking sheet and gently spread the cream cheese onto the dough, leaving a 3/4-inch-wide border. Spread the fig mixture over the cream cheese and fold the border edge over the fig mixture to form the crostata.

3. Top the crostata with the prosciutto strips and lightly brush the folded edge of the dough with the egg white. Bake until golden—about 15 minutes. Cool on the sheet for 10 to 15 minutes before serving.

NUTRITION PER SERVING: calories: 380; protein: 6 g; fat: 23 g; carbohydrate: 37 g; fiber: 3 g; sodium: 600 mg; cholesterol: 16 mg

< 48 >

< **49** >

Caramelized-Onion and Gruyère Tarts

These ready-to-bake tarts answer the question of what to serve drop-in visitors. You need only plan ahead for reheating time. Add a sprinkling of fresh herbs, a bottle of wine, and a simple green salad to make the meal feel special.

MAKES: 8 TARTS (16 SERVINGS)

3 cups (about 10 ounces) grated Gruyère cheese

8 ounces (1 package) cream cheese, softened

1 tablespoon Dijon mustard

1 tablespoon chopped fresh oregano

3/4 teaspoon ground black pepper

2 tablespoons unsalted butter

2 large sweet yellow onions, sliced 1/4 inch thick (2 cups)

2 tablespoon fresh thyme

1 recipe Quick Puff Pastry (page 41)

1/2 cup Kalamata olives, sliced

1. Preheat the oven to 400°F (if you plan to freeze the tarts, do not preheat, and omit step 3 below). Mix the Gruyère, cream cheese, mustard, oregano, and pepper in a small bowl and set aside. Melt the butter in a large skillet over medium-low heat, add the onions, and cook, stirring occasionally, until dark brown and caramelized—about 1 hour. Stir in the thyme and set aside.

2. With a sharp knife, cut the puff pastry dough into 8 equal-sized pieces. Roll each piece out into an 8-by-6-inch rectangle. Spread about 1/4 cup of the cheese mixture on each piece of dough, leaving a 1/2-inch border. Top with 1/4 cup caramelized onions and 1 tablespoon olives. Place the tarts on parchment-lined baking pans.

3. Bake the tarts for 10 minutes, then reduce the oven temperature to 375°F and continue baking until they are puffed and golden—about 12 minutes longer.

4. To freeze the tarts before baking them: Cover the tarts on the baking pan with plastic wrap and freeze until they are solid—about 2 hours. Wrap each tart securely in freezer paper or aluminum foil; stack them in an airtight container. Store the frozen tarts for up to 2 months. To serve, bake the frozen tarts at 400°F for 12 minutes, reduce the oven temperature to 375°F, and continue baking until puffed and golden—about 15 minutes longer.

NUTRITION PER SERVING: calories: 430; protein: 11 g; fat: 32 g; carbohydrate: 3 g; fiber: 2 g; sodium: 311 mg; cholesterol: 106 mg

Pesto-Ricotta Quiche

This is the perfect pie to make when fresh basil is abundant. And the crust could not be easier: Store-bought frozen phyllo dough—rolled very thin and layered to create a light and flaky pastry—is pressed into a pie tin to create a casual crust for the egg and cheese filling. For photo, see page 38.

MAKES: ONE 9-INCH PIE (8 SERVINGS)

6 tablespoons unsalted butter

1 large leek, trimmed, washed, and thinly sliced

2 large eggs

2 large egg whites

1/4 cup heavy cream

1 cup ricotta

1/2 cup grated Parmesan cheese

3 tablespoons Chunky Chopped Pesto (recipe follows)

2 tablespoons finely chopped fresh parsley leaves

1/4 teaspoon salt

1/4 teaspoon ground black pepper

8 frozen phyllo sheets, thawed

1. Preheat the oven to 375°F. Lightly butter a 9-inch pie pan and set aside. Melt 2 tablespoons butter in a medium-size skillet over medium-high heat. Add the leeks and cook, stirring often, until soft, 5 to 7 minutes. Transfer to a large bowl to cool.

2. Meanwhile, whisk the eggs, egg whites, and cream together in a medium-size bowl and add to the leeks, along with the ricotta, Parmesan, pesto, parsley, salt, and pepper. Stir to combine and set aside. Melt the remaining 4 tablespoons butter in a small bowl.

3. Lay one sheet of phyllo in the prepared pie pan. Brush the phyllo with melted butter, leaving a 1 1/2-inch rim unbrushed. Lay a second sheet of phyllo on the first and butter it the same way. Repeat with the remaining sheets of phyllo.

4. Using kitchen shears, trim the edges of the phyllo to roughly conform to the shape of the pie pan, then pour in the filling. Brush the top of the phyllo rim with butter, and bake until the edges are golden brown and the filling is set, about 40 minutes. Transfer to wire rack to cool. Serve warm.

★ ★ ★

Chunky Chopped Pesto

When fresh basil is abundant, make a big batch of this homemade pesto. Portion some into jars to give away, and freeze the rest in ice-cube trays to use later on pasta, pizza, or bruschetta.

7 1/2 cups fresh basil leaves

1 1/2 cups extra-virgin olive oil

3 cloves garlic

1 teaspoon coarse salt

1/2 teaspoon ground black pepper

3/4 cup toasted pine nuts

3/4 cup grated Parmesan cheese

Puree the basil, oil, garlic, salt, and pepper in a food processor. Add the pine nuts and Parmesan and pulse until the nuts are roughly chopped.

NUTRITION PER SERVING OF QUICHE: calories: 330; protein: 10 g; fat: 26 g; carbohydrate: 13 g; fiber: 1 g; sodium: 555 mg; cholesterol: 118 mg

single-crust pies

DECORATIVE BORDERS

Once you've mastered the basics, rolling and shaping a pie crust is a relaxing—and rewarding!—endeavor. Essential Techniques (page 17) summarizes the basic steps, while Pie Baker's Cheat Sheet (page 21) offers additional pointers. Here we provide some ideas for decorative edges to finish off your single-crust pies in style. They can also be used on double-crust pies; see page 81 for recipe list.

Prepare the dough for the Baked Pie Shell (page 59). For best results, chill the pie dough before you begin; that makes it easier to work with. Roll it and place it in the pan using a rolling pin, as described on page 17. Then create one of the ornamental borders illustrated below. If the decorative pie edges appear to be overbrowning in the oven, cover them with strips of aluminum foil, or create an aluminum foil circle that covers the crust only.

FORKED: This is the quickest, easiest border, but it gives piecrusts a finished look none-the-less. Using kitchen shears, trim the dough edge even with the rim of the pan. With floured fork tines, press the dough to the rim of plate. Repeat all the way around to create a grooved pattern.

FLUTED: Using kitchen shears, trim the dough to leave a 1-inch overhang. Fold this under and pinch to make a stand-up edge. Push the tip of one index finger against the outside of the rim; with the index finger and thumb of the other hand, press to make a ruffle. Repeat all the way around, leaving about ¼ inch between the ruffles.

CRIMPED: Using kitchen shears, trim the dough to leave a 1-inch overhang. Fold this under and pinch to make a stand-up edge. Push the tip of one index finger against the inside of the rim, then pinch the dough by pressing with the index finger and thumb of the other hand. Repeat, moving your outer index finger into the impression made by your thumb.

TURRET: Using kitchen shears, trim the dough to leave a 1-inch overhang. Fold this under and pinch to make a stand-up edge. With a small knife, make cuts down through the edge to the rim of the pie pan, spacing cuts ½ inch apart. Fold pieces alternately toward the center and the rim.

HEARTS OR LEAVES: Using kitchen shears, trim the dough edge even with the rim of the pan. Gather the trimmings and roll them out ⅛ inch thick. With a knife or tiny cookie cutter, cut out leaves or hearts of equal size. Lightly brush the edge of the piecrust with water, then press the cutouts onto it all around the pie. (If you want even more dough to decorate with, prepare Grandma's Pie Dough, page 85, for a double-crust pie.)

Baked Pie Shell

This dependable recipe is used for several of the pies
in this chapter. Feel free to substitute it in any recipe
calling for a blind-baked store-bought 9-inch crust.

MAKES: ONE 9-INCH PIECRUST (8 SERVINGS)

1¼ **cups all-purpose flour**

¼ **teaspoon salt**

½ **cup (1 stick) unsalted butter, chilled and cut into small pieces**

4 to 6 **tablespoons ice water**

1. Combine the flour and salt in a large bowl. Cut in the butter using a pastry blender, 2 knives, or your fingers until the mixture resembles coarse meal. Sprinkle the ice water over the flour mixture 1 tablespoon at a time and mix with your hands or a fork until just combined. Transfer the dough to a clean, lightly floured work surface, gently gather it together, and flatten it into a disk. Wrap the dough in plastic; chill it for at least 1 hour or up to overnight. (The chilled dough may be frozen for up to 3 months.)

2. Preheat the oven to 450°F and position the rack in the center. On a lightly floured surface, roll the dough into a round about ⅛ inch thick. Transfer the round to a 9-inch pie pan, gently fit it into the pan. Trim and finish the edge using one of the techniques described in Decorative Borders, pages 56 to 57.

3. Prick the bottom and sides of the dough with a fork, then line it with parchment paper and fill it with dried beans or pie weights. Bake the shell until it is lightly browned—10 to 12 minutes. Transfer to a wire rack to cool completely.

NUTRITION PER ⅛ RECIPE: calories: 170; protein: 2 g; fat: 122 g; carbohydrate: 15 g; fiber: 0.5 g; sodium: 75 mg; cholesterol: 30 mg

Orange Meringue Pie

This old-fashioned pie makes a great gift. Present it in
a vintage tin lined with waxed or tissue paper. Fill in and attach
a recipe card; see the back of the book for options.

MAKES: ONE 9-INCH PIE (8 SERVINGS)

< **60** >

- 2 cups sugar
- 3 tablespoons all-purpose flour
- 3 1/2 tablespoons cornstarch
- 1/4 teaspoon salt
- 1/2 cup orange juice concentrate
- 3 tablespoons fresh lemon juice
- 1 1/2 cups water
- 2 tablespoons unsalted butter
- 4 eggs, separated
- 1 Baked Pie Shell (page 59)
- 1 teaspoon pure vanilla extract
- 1/2 teaspoon cream of tartar

1. Whisk 1 1/2 cups sugar together with the flour, cornstarch, and salt in a large saucepan. Add the juice concentrate, lemon juice, and water. Bring the mixture to a boil, whisking continuously. Whisk in the butter and remove the pan from the heat.

Louisiana

2. Lightly beat the egg yolks in a medium-size bowl. Drizzle in 1/2 cup hot juice mixture while whisking the yolks, then slowly pour the yolk mixture into the juice mixture in the saucepan. Cook over medium-low heat until the filling is very thick and glossy— about 5 minutes. Pour it through a strainer into the prepared pie shell and set aside.

colador

3. Preheat the oven to 350°F. Beat the egg whites, vanilla, and cream of tartar to soft peaks using a handheld mixer set on medium speed. Increase the mixer speed to high, gradually add the remaining 1/2 cup sugar, and continue to beat until stiff peaks form. Gently spread the meringue over the hot filling, taking care to spread it to the edges of the crust all around (see Tip). Use a spoon to make a pattern of dips and peaks on the surface of the meringue. Bake until the meringue is lightly browned—about 10 minutes. Transfer to a wire rack to cool completely.

TIP: To prevent the meringue topping from shrinking, make sure it touches the crust. It will "grab" the edges while it browns.

NUTRITION PER SERVING: calories: 483; protein: 6 g; fat: 17 g; carbohydrate: 78 g; fiber: 1 g; sodium: 184 mg; cholesterol: 143 mg

< 61 >

Lemon Meringue Pie

This classic dessert has delighted American families since the early 1800s. For voluminous meringue, bring the egg whites to room temperature before whipping them and make certain your whisk and bowl are very clean. The dough contains vegetable shortening for an extra-flakey crust.

MAKES: ONE 9-INCH PIE (8 SERVINGS)

2 1/4 cups all-purpose flour

1 1/4 cups plus 7 tablespoons sugar

1/4 teaspoon salt

15 tablespoons unsalted butter, chilled and cut into small pieces

1/4 cup vegetable shortening, chilled

4 to 6 tablespoons ice water

5 tablespoons cornstarch

1 1/2 cups water

1/2 cup fresh lemon juice (from about 3 lemons)

1 tablespoon finely grated lemon zest

3 large eggs, separated

1. Combine the flour, 2 tablespoons sugar, and salt in a large bowl. Cut in 12 tablespoons butter and the shortening using a pastry blender, 2 knives, or your fingers until the mixture resembles coarse meal. Stir in the ice water 1 tablespoon at a time until the dough just holds together when pressed. Transfer the dough to a lightly floured work surface, gather it together, and flatten it into a disk. Wrap the dough in plastic and chill it for at least 1 hour or up to overnight. (The chilled dough may be frozen for up to 3 months.)

2. Preheat the oven to 425°F. On a lightly floured surface, roll the dough into a circle 1/8 inch thick and fit it gently into a 9-inch pie pan. Trim away the excess dough, leaving a 1/2-inch overhang. Fold the edges under and crimp them along the rim. Prick the bottom of the dough several times with a fork, line it with parchment paper, and fill it with beans or pie weights. Bake for 15 minutes. Remove the paper and weights and bake for 15 more minutes. Transfer to a

wire rack to cool completely. Reduce the oven temperature to 350°F.

3. Meanwhile, whisk the cornstarch, 1 1/4 cups sugar, and water together in a medium-size saucepan. Add the lemon juice, zest, and egg yolks; cook the mixture over medium heat, stirring constantly, until it begins to bubble and thicken—about 10 minutes. Remove the lemon curd from the heat, whisk in the remaining 3 tablespoons butter, and pour it through a strainer into the prepared crust.

4. Beat the egg whites to soft peaks. Add the remaining 5 tablespoons sugar in a slow, steady stream, and continue to beat until the whites have increased in volume about six times and are glossy and firm. (They will make pointy peaks when the beaters or whisk are lifted.)

5. Spread the meringue over the filling, taking care to spread the edges of the crust all around. Bake until the meringue is golden brown—10 to 15 minutes. Transfer to a wire rack to cool completely.

NUTRITION PER SERVING: calories: 586; protein: 6 g; fat: 29 g; carbohydrate: 76 g; fiber: 1 g; sodium: 101 mg; cholesterol

< **63** >

Fresh Berry Crumble Pie

This deep-dish summer berry pie features a hazelnut crust and a brown-sugar hazelnut crumb topping. Top with a dollop of whipped cream for a dessert worthy of a country fair ribbon.

MAKES: ONE 9-INCH DEEP-DISH PIE (12 SERVINGS)

13 tablespoons unsalted butter, chilled and cubed

1 3/4 cups confectioners' sugar, sifted

1 cup hazelnuts, finely ground

1/4 teaspoon salt

1/2 teaspoon pure vanilla extract

1 large egg

2 cups all-purpose flour

3 quarts strawberries, hulled and halved

1 tablespoon fresh lemon juice

3 tablespoons cornstarch

1/2 pint (1 cup) raspberries

1/4 cup light brown sugar

1. In the bowl of a mixer fitted with the paddle attachment, beat 10 tablespoons butter on high speed until creamy. Reduce the speed to low and add 1 cup confectioners' sugar and 1/2 cup hazelnuts, along with the salt, vanilla, and egg; beat until smooth. Add 1 2/3 cups flour in 3 additions, mixing until just combined. Gather the dough into a ball, wrap it in plastic, and chill it for at least 4 hours.

2. Combine the remaining 3/4 cup confectioners' sugar and the strawberries in a large skillet over medium-high heat and cook until the strawberries just begin to soften—about 7 minutes. Transfer the berries to a medium-size bowl, cover with plastic wrap, and set aside for 45 minutes.

3. Strain the berry juice into the skillet and simmer it over high heat until it is thickened and reduced to about 3/4 cup. Combine the strawberries, lemon juice, cornstarch, and reduced syrup in a large bowl, fold in the raspberries, and set the mixture aside. Place the

< **64** >

brown sugar, with the remaining butter, hazelnuts, and flour, in a food processor and pulse just to combine. Set aside.

4. Preheat the oven to 400°F. On a lightly floured surface, between two sheets of waxed paper, roll the dough into a round at least 12 inches in diameter and about $\frac{1}{16}$ inch thick; transfer the dough to a pie plate. Line the shell with parchment paper and fill it with dried beans or pie weights. Bake the shell until it is lightly browned— about 15 minutes. Remove the paper and beans; bake for 10 minutes longer. Transfer to a wire rack to cool completely.

5. Fill the pie shell with the berry mixture and top it with the hazelnut crumble. Cover the edges of the crust with strips of foil, place the pie on a baking sheet, and bake until the filling bubbles— about 40 minutes. Transfer to a wire rack to cool completely.

NUTRITION PER SERVING: calories: 350; protein: 5 g; fat: 20 g; carbohydrate: 41 g; fiber: 4 g; sodium: 50 mg; cholesterol: 51 mg

< **65** >

Pumpkin-Pecan Pie

Why not serve two favorites in a single pie? Guests will be surprised to find a creamy pumpkin filling beneath what appears to be a traditional pecan pie. Be forewarned: This pie is so rich, small slices will satisfy even the most ardent dessert enthusiasts. This recipe makes two pies—perfect for holiday festivities.

MAKES: TWO 9-INCH PIES (24 SERVINGS)

CRUST

2 cups unsifted all-purpose flour

3/4 cup (1 1/2 sticks) unsalted butter, chilled

6 to 7 tablespoons ice water

PUMPKIN LAYER

2 large eggs, separated

1/2 cup sugar

1 (16-ounce) can pumpkin, or 2 cups well-drained fresh pumpkin puree

1/2 cup half-and-half

2 teaspoons pumpkin pie spice

1/2 teaspoon salt

PECAN LAYER

3 tablespoons unsalted butter

1/2 cup sugar

1 cup dark corn syrup

1 teaspoon pure vanilla extract

2 large eggs

2 cups pecan halves

1. **For the crust:** Put the flour in a large bowl. Cut in the butter using a pastry blender, 2 knives, or your fingers until the mixture resembles coarse meal. Sprinkle in the ice water, 1 tablespoon at a time, tossing lightly after each addition, just until the pastry holds together. Divide the dough in half and shape each piece into a disk. Wrap each disk in plastic and refrigerate for at least 1 hour.

2. On a lightly floured surface, roll one disk into a 12-inch round. Gently fit the dough into a 9-inch pie pan, fold the overhang inward, and form a high fluted edge. Repeat with the other pastry disk; refrigerate while you prepare the pumpkin filling. Preheat the oven to 350°F.

3. **For the pumpkin layer:** In a small bowl, using a handheld mixer on high speed, beat the egg whites until soft peaks form. In a large bowl, with the same beaters and the mixer on low speed, beat the egg yolks, sugar, pumpkin, half-and-half, spice, and salt until blended. With a rubber spatula, fold the egg whites into the pumpkin mixture. Divide the filling between the two pie shells and bake for 30 minutes.

4. Meanwhile, prepare the pecan layer: In a 1-quart saucepan over low heat, melt the butter. Remove the pan from the heat and stir in the sugar, corn syrup, and vanilla. Beat in the eggs.

5. Carefully arrange the pecans in a single layer on top of the pumpkin layer in a decorative pattern. Pour the sugar mixture over the pecans, taking care not to disturb them.

6. Return the pies to the oven and bake until a knife inserted 1 inch from the edge comes out clean—15 to 20 minutes longer. Transfer to a wire rack to cool completely. Gently cover and chill.

NUTRITION PER SERVING: calories: 255; protein: 3 g; fat: 15 g; carbohydrate: 30g; fiber: 2 g; sodium: 85 mg; cholesterol: 56 mg

Butterscotch Pie

Your friends and family will adore this sweet custard pie.
Dress it up with a sprinkle of toasted nuts or grated chocolate.
For a winning wedge, always slice cream or custard pies when
they are well-chilled, wiping the knife between cuts.

MAKES: ONE 9-INCH PIE (8 SERVINGS)

- ½ **cup (1 stick) unsalted butter**
- 1¼ **cups light brown sugar**
- 1½ **cups hot water**
- ¼ **cup cornstarch**
- **3 tablespoons all-purpose flour**
- ½ **teaspoon salt**
- 1½ **cups heavy cream**
- ½ **cup whole milk**
- **4 egg yolks**
- **1 teaspoon pure vanilla extract**
- **1 Baked Pie Shell (page 59)**
- **1 teaspoon honey**
- **2 tablespoons confectioners' sugar**
- ¼ **cup toasted almond slices, optional**

1. Melt the butter in a medium-size saucepan over medium heat until it begins to brown. Stir in the brown sugar. Add the hot water and whisk until the mixture comes to a boil. Continue to cook for 2 more minutes; remove the pan from the heat and set aside.

2. Combine the cornstarch, flour, and salt in a small bowl. Whisk in ½ cup cream and the milk until smooth; pour this into the butter mixture. Whisk continuously, over medium heat, until the mixture comes to a boil and thickens— about 3 minutes. Remove the pan from the heat. Lightly beat the egg yolks together in a medium-size bowl. Stream in ½ cup of the hot mixture while whisking the yolks. Whisk the egg mixture into the milk mixture in the saucepan and cook over medium heat for 1 minute. Pour the custard through a strainer into a bowl and stir in the vanilla. Pour the custard into the prepared pie shell and chill until set.

3. Beat the remaining 1 cup cream with the honey and confectioners' sugar until stiff peaks form. Spread the cream over the cooled pie and chill. Sprinkle with toasted almonds, if desired, before serving.

NUTRITION PER SERVING: calories: 630; protein: 5 g; fat: 42 g; carbohydrate: 59 g; fiber: 1 g; sodium: 263 mg; cholesterol: 225 mg

Mississippi Mud Pie

The Crown Restaurant in Indianola, Mississippi, created this mud pie with a layer of chocolate custard, vanilla ice cream, and a drizzle of rich fudge sauce. Here we use a store-bought piecrust for ease. (You can also use the Baked Pie Shell on page 59 and skip step 1 of the instructions.) According to folklore, the Delta region's beloved chocolate pie was so named because its fudgy base resembles the muddy bottom of the Mississippi River.

MAKES: ONE 9-INCH PIE (8 SERVINGS)

1 (9-inch) store-bought piecrust

½ cup (1 stick) unsalted butter, softened

1¾ cups sugar

¼ cup cocoa

¼ cup all-purpose flour

4 large eggs, beaten

1 teaspoon pure vanilla extract

3 cups vanilla or mocha ice cream, slightly softened

3 tablespoons fudge sauce

1. Preheat the oven to 450°F. Line the unbaked crust with parchment paper and fill it with dried beans or pie weights; bake until the dough is lightly golden and set—10 to 15 minutes. Cool the crust on a wire rack. Reduce the oven temperature to 350°F.

2. In a bowl, stir together the butter, sugar, and cocoa until well combined. Add the flour, eggs, and vanilla and mix until smooth. Pour the filling into the prepared crust and bake for 30 to 40 minutes.

3. Transfer to a wire rack to cool completely. Gently mound ice cream over the pie and freeze until the ice cream sets. Drizzle with fudge sauce before serving.

NUTRITION PER SERVING: calories: 560; protein: 7 g; fat: 26 g; carbohydrate: 76 g; fiber: 2 g; sodium: 185 mg; cholesterol: 158 mg

Shoofly Pie

This shoofly pie, from the Bird-in-Hand Bakery in Lancaster County, Pennsylvania, is a regional classic. In the late eighteenth century, enterprising Pennsylvania-Dutch cooks baked this rich molasses pie whenever fruit was in short supply. A brown-sugar-and-cinnamon topping decorates this version.

MAKES: ONE 9-INCH PIE (8 SERVINGS)

CRUST

2 cups all-purpose flour

1 teaspoon salt

$^3/_4$ cup vegetable shortening, chilled

5 tablespoons ice water

FILLING

$^1/_2$ cup dark corn syrup

$^1/_4$ cup light brown sugar, packed

1 large egg, beaten

$^1/_2$ teaspoon baking soda

$^1/_2$ cup hot water

CRUMB TOPPING

1 cup all-purpose flour

3 tablespoons vegetable shortening

$^2/_3$ cup light brown sugar, packed

1 pinch salt

1 pinch ground cinnamon

1. **For the crust:** In a medium-size bowl, mix the flour and salt. Cut into the shortening using a pastry blender, 2 knives, or your fingers until the mixture resembles coarse meal. Gradually add the ice water until combined. Press the dough together into a disk, wrap it in plastic, and chill for at least 1 hour or up to overnight. On a lightly floured surface, roll the dough into a round about $^1/_8$ inch thick; gently fit the dough round into a 9-inch pie pan. Preheat the oven to 350°F.

2. **For the filling:** Combine the corn syrup, brown sugar, and egg. Dissolve the baking soda in the hot water, stir it into the syrup mixture, and pour the filling into the crust.

3. **For the crumb topping:** In a medium-size bowl, mix the flour, shortening, brown sugar, salt, and cinnamon using your fingers or a pastry blender until combined. Sprinkle the crumbs evenly over the pie filling.

4. Bake the pie for 50 to 60 minutes, or until the filling is set. Transfer to a wire rack to cool completely.

NUTRITION PER SERVING: calories: 546; protein: 6 g; fat: 6 g; carbohydrate: 76 g; fiber: 1 g; sodium: 436 mg; cholesterol: 26 mg

Apple-Cheddar Crumble Pie

This single-crust pie is finished with a Cheddar cheese–enriched crumble topping. Choose an assortment of tart and sweet apple varieties to yield a heavenly perfumed pie. For photo, see page 20.

MAKES: ONE 9-INCH PIE (12 SERVINGS)

CRUST

1 1/4 cups all-purpose flour

1/2 teaspoon salt

1/8 teaspoon ground red pepper (cayenne)

1/2 cup (1 stick) unsalted butter, chilled and cut into pieces

3/4 cup grated sharp Cheddar cheese

3 to 4 tablespoons ice water

FILLING

3 medium-size tart apples, such as Rhode Island Greening, Cortland, or Granny Smith, peeled, cored, and thinly sliced (3 cups)

3 medium-size sweet apples, such as Rome Beauty or Jonathan, peeled, cored, and thinly sliced (3 cups)

1 teaspoon grated lemon zest

1/4 cup fresh lemon juice (from about 2 lemons)

3/4 cup sugar

2 tablespoons all-purpose flour

1/2 teaspoon ground cinnamon

1/4 teaspoon salt

1/4 teaspoon ground nutmeg

1/8 teaspoon ground allspice

CRUMBLE TOPPING

1/3 cup all-purpose flour

3 tablespoons brown sugar, packed

3 tablespoons unsalted butter, chilled and cut into small pieces

1/2 cup grated sharp Cheddar cheese

1. **For the crust:** In a large bowl, combine the flour, salt, and ground red pepper. Cut in the butter using a pastry blender, 2 knives, or your fingers until the mixture resembles coarse meal. Add the cheese and toss. Add the ice water, 1 tablespoon at a time, until a rough dough forms. Gather the dough together, shape it into a $3/4$-inch-thick disk, and tightly wrap it in plastic. Refrigerate for 30 minutes.

2. On a lightly floured surface, roll the dough into an 11-inch circle about $1/4$ inch thick. Gently fit it into a 9-inch pie pan, turn the overhanging dough under to form an edge along the top of the pan, and crimp the edge. Chill for 30 minutes.

3. Preheat the oven to 425°F and place the rack in the center position. Line the crust with parchment paper and fill it with pie weights or dried beans. Bake until the crust is lightly browned— about 15 minutes. Transfer to a wire rack and remove the weights and paper. Leave the oven on.

4. **For the filling:** In a large bowl, toss all the apple slices with the lemon zest and juice. In a small bowl, mix the sugar, flour, cinnamon, salt, nutmeg, and allspice. Sprinkle the spice mixture over the apples and toss to mix thoroughly. Spoon the apples into the prepared crust.

5. **For the crumble topping:** In a small bowl, with a fork, toss the flour, brown sugar, butter, and grated cheese. Sprinkle the top of the pie with the crumble mixture.

6. Bake the pie until the topping is golden brown—50 to 60 minutes. Transfer to a wire rack to cool for at least 30 minutes. Serve warm or at room temperature.

NUTRITION PER SERVING: calories: 366; protein: 6 g; fat: 18 g; carbohydrate: 47 g; fiber: 13 g; sodium: 251 mg; cholesterol: 498 mg

Tomato and Cheese Pie

Here pie takes a savory turn with a ripe tomato and cheese filling seasoned with fresh chopped basil. Use a serrated knife to slice it.

MAKES: ONE 9-INCH PIE (8 SERVINGS)

4 medium plum tomatoes

1 (9-inch) store-bought deep-dish pie shell, prebaked according to package directions

1 cup finely chopped white onion

1/2 teaspoon salt

1/2 teaspoon ground black pepper

2 tablespoons chopped fresh basil

1/2 cup mayonnaise

1/2 cup grated Parmesan cheese

1 cup grated Cheddar cheese

1. Preheat the oven to 375°F. Cut 6 nice slices from one of the tomatoes and set them aside for garnish. Halve the remaining tomatoes, remove the seeds, and cut each half into about 6 wedges.

2. Arrange half of the tomato wedges in the bottom of the pie shell. Sprinkle with 1/2 cup onion, 1/4 teaspoon each salt and pepper, and 1 tablespoon basil.

3. Stir together the mayonnaise, Parmesan, and Cheddar in a small bowl, then dab half of this mixture over the onion layer. Repeat the layering to use the remaining tomatoes, onion, salt, pepper, and basil. Add the remaining mayonnaise mixture. Arrange the reserved tomato slices in a pinwheel design at the center of the pie.

4. Bake for 30 to 40 minutes, until golden brown. If the crust starts to overbrown, cover the edges with aluminum foil. Transfer to a wire rack to cool for 20 minutes. Serve warm.

NUTRITION PER SERVING: calories: 273; protein: 7 g; fat: 22 g; carbohydrate: 12 g; fiber: 1 g; sodium: 499 mg; cholesterol: 23 mg

Whole-Wheat Spinach and Tofu Quiche

Tahini and toasted sesame seeds impart a nutty flavor
to this vegan spinach pie. Serve it hot from the oven
or at room temperature. Feel free to substitute its wholesome
whole-wheat crust in the Tomato and Cheese Pie recipe on page 76,
or in other savory pies or quiches containing dairy.

MAKES: ONE 9-INCH PIE (8 SERVINGS)

WHOLE-WHEAT CRUST

1 cup unsifted all-purpose flour

¹/₂ cup whole-wheat flour

¹/₂ teaspoon salt

¹/₃ cup canola oil or light olive oil

3 tablespoons ice water

FILLING

1 tablespoon cold-pressed or refined (not toasted) sesame oil or peanut oil

3 cloves garlic, chopped

1 medium onion, chopped

1 teaspoon Worcestershire sauce, or 2 or 3 drops hot red pepper sauce

1 pound fresh spinach leaves, tough stems removed (12 cups loosely packed), or two 20-ounce packages frozen spinach, thawed and well drained

1 tablespoon cornstarch

3 tablespoons water

1 (10-ounce) container soft tofu, drained

2 tablespoons tahini

¹/₂ teaspoon salt

¹/₄ teaspoon ground black pepper

¹/₈ teaspoon ground nutmeg

1 teaspoon sesame seeds, toasted (optional)

Sweet red pepper strips (optional)

1. **For the crust:** Preheat the oven to 400°F. In a large bowl, combine the flours and salt; stir in the oil. Add the ice water, 1 tablespoon at a time, just until the pastry holds together when lightly pressed into a ball.

2. Place the dough between 2 lightly floured sheets of waxed paper and roll it into a 10-inch round. Peel off one piece of waxed paper, then fit the pastry into a 9-inch pie plate and remove the second sheet. Trim the edge of the dough even with the rim of the plate, and crimp it with the tines of a fork. Line the pastry with aluminum foil and fill it with pie weights or dried beans. Bake the pastry for 10 minutes. Transfer to a wire rack and remove the weights and foil. Reduce the oven temperature to 375°F.

3. **Meanwhile, prepare the filling:** In a 5-quart Dutch oven, heat the oil. Add the garlic and onion and sauté until the onion is transparent. Add the Worcestershire sauce and spinach and cover the Dutch oven tightly with its lid. Cook for 2 minutes. Stir the spinach and continue cooking, covered, for 2 minutes longer. In a small bowl, stir together the cornstarch and water. Add the cornstarch mixture to the Dutch oven. Remove the pot from the heat and let it cool slightly.

4. In a food processor fitted with a chopping blade, process the spinach mixture until it is coarsely chopped. In a medium-size bowl, use a fork to stir together the spinach mixture, tofu, tahini, salt, pepper, and nutmeg. Pour the filling into the pastry shell.

5. Bake the pie until the top is light golden brown—about 30 minutes. Transfer to a wire rack to cool. Sprinkle it with toasted sesame seeds and garnish with the red pepper strips, if desired. Serve warm.

NUTRITION PER SERVING: calories: 250; protein: 7 g; fat: 15 g; carbohydrate: 23 g; fiber: 3 g; sodium: 333 mg; cholesterol: 0 mg

double-crust pies

PEEP TOPS AND LATTICES

A double-crust pie is a country classic: Half the dough is used to line the pie pan, while the other half tops the filling, encasing its goodness with a flaky golden-brown lid. If you adore piecrust, then double-crust pies are worth mastering!

For an overview of how to roll and shape your pie, see Essential Techniques (page 17). For quick pie-baking tips, see Pie Baker's Cheat Sheet (page 21).

Here we provide some clever ideas for decorative tops to finish off your double-crust pies in style. First, prepare the recipe for Grandma's Pie Dough (page 85).

For best results, chill the dough before you begin to make it easier to work with. Roll a disk of the dough into a 12-inch round and line the pie pan as described on page 17; add your filling. Roll a second disk of dough into another 12-inch round; place it over the filling. Trim the edge with kitchen shears, leaving a 1-inch overhang; pinch to make a high edge and create a fluted or crimped edge, as described on page 56 or 57. Reserve the trimmings.

WINDOW: Cut a 4-inch ✕ in the center of the top crust; fold back the points to create a square opening. This window is not only decorative; it will also allow steam to escape from the pie during baking. Feel free to experiment with making windows in other whimsical shapes, such as the multiple tiny stars cut out of the top crust of the Strawberry Rhubarb Pie (page 96).

APPLIQUÉ: Roll out the reserved trimmings. Use a cookie cutter or a small knife to cut free-form shapes, such as fruits, hearts, or leaves (try using the back of the knife to mark veins on the leaves); brush the cutouts with water, then place them, wet side down, on top of the pie. Cut several 1-inch slits in the top crust to allow steam to escape. The Quince Mince Pie (page 104) uses leaf-shaped appliqués cut from its own top crust as decoration.

SIMPLE LATTICE: Roll the second disk of dough into a 12-inch round, but instead of placing it over the filling, use a knife or fluted pastry wheel to cut it into ½-inch strips. Moisten the edge of bottom crust with water. Place pastry strips about 1 inch apart across pie; press each strip at both ends to seal. Repeat with an equal number of strips placed at right angles to the first ones to create a lattice design. Turn overhang up over the ends of the strips; pinch to seal. Make a high, stand-up edge that will hold the juices in, then flute the edge (see page 56).

WOVEN LATTICE: Follow the instructions for the simple lattice above, but when you place the first layer of strips on pie, do not seal the ends. Fold every other strip back halfway from the center of pie. Place center cross strip on pie and replace folded part of strips. Now fold back alternate strips; position second cross strip in place. Repeat until you've woven all the cross strips into a lattice pattern. Seal ends and make a high, fluted edge.

Grandma's Pie Dough

This recipe produces a flaky, golden crust that is used in several of the recipes in this chapter. Feel free to substitute it in any recipe calling for a 9-inch double crust. Instead of simply pricking the top crust with a fork as described in step 3, if you like, you can follow the instructions for one of the decorative tops on pages 82 to 83.

MAKES: 4 SINGLE CRUSTS

4 cups all-purpose flour

$3/4$ teaspoon salt

1 tablespoon sugar

$1^3/4$ cups ($3^1/2$ sticks) unsalted butter, chilled and cut into small pieces

1 tablespoon white vinegar

1 large egg

$1/2$ cup ice water

1. Combine the flour, salt, and sugar in a large bowl. Cut in the butter using a pastry blender, 2 knives, or your fingers until the mixture resembles coarse meal.

2. Whisk the vinegar, egg, and ice water together and mix the liquid into the flour mixture with your hands until just combined. Transfer the dough to a clean work surface and gently press to form a mass.

3. Divide the dough into 4 equal parts. Shape each into a disk and wrap it in plastic. Chill for at least 1 hour or freeze extras for up to 3 months.

NUTRITION PER $1/8$ SINGLE CRUST: calories: 150; protein: 2 g; fat 10 g; carbohydrate: 13 g; fiber: 0 g; sodium: 59 mg; cholesterol: 34 mg

Farmhouse Apple Pie

This is the sort of apple pie Grandma used to make—that is, if you were lucky! Enjoy it warm or cold, unembellished or à la mode.

MAKES ONE 9-INCH PIE (8 SERVINGS)

½ recipe (2 disks) Grandma's Pie Dough (page 85)

2½ pounds mixed apples, peeled, cored, and chopped into ¾-inch pieces

2 tablespoons all-purpose flour

¾ cup plus 1 tablespoon sugar

1 teaspoon ground cinnamon

¼ teaspoon ground nutmeg

½ teaspoon salt

1 tablespoon fresh lemon juice

1. Preheat the oven to 375°F. On a lightly floured surface, roll the disks of dough into rounds about ⅛ inch thick; transfer one to a 9-inch pie pan (see Tip). Place the remaining round on a baking sheet lined with parchment paper; keep both dough pieces chilled.

2. Toss the apples, flour, ¾ cup sugar, cinnamon, nutmeg, salt, and lemon juice together and mix until combined. Pour the apple mixture into the prepared pie pan and place the top dough round over it. Trim the edges of the dough, leaving a ½-inch overhang; fold that under and crimp the edges. Sprinkle the top of the pie with the remaining 1 tablespoon sugar; chill for 10 minutes.

3. Bake until the fruit is bubbling and the crust is golden brown—50 to 55 minutes. Transfer to a wire rack to cool completely.

TIP: Drape the dough over the rolling pin and unroll it onto the pie pan to prevent tearing.

NUTRITION PER SERVING: calories: 456; protein: 4.5 g; fat: 21 g; carbohydrate: 66 g; fiber: 3 g; sodium: 264 mg; cholesterol: 68 mg

Mini Cherry Pies

These sweet-tart pies will charm anyone who takes a bite.

MAKES: TWO 4-INCH PIES (4 SERVINGS)

1 cup all-purpose flour

3 tablespoons dark brown sugar

5/8 teaspoon salt

7 tablespoons unsalted butter, chilled

3 tablespoons ice water

1 pound sweet or sour cherries (about 3 cups), pitted

3 tablespoons (for sweet cherries) or 2/3 cup (for sour) granulated sugar

2 tablespoons cornstarch

1 tablespoon fresh lemon juice

2 teaspoons lemon zest

1. Combine the flour, brown sugar, and 1/8 teaspoon salt in a large bowl. Cut in 6 tablespoons butter using a pastry blender, 2 knives, or your fingers until the mixture resembles coarse meal. Add the ice water 1 tablespoon at a time, tossing with a fork just until combined. Pat the dough into a 5-by-6-inch rectangle, cover it tightly with plastic wrap, and chill for at least 30 minutes.

2. Preheat the oven to 350°F. Melt the remaining butter and combine it in a bowl with the cherries, granulated sugar, cornstarch, lemon juice and zest, and remaining salt; set aside. Divide the dough into 4 equal pieces and roll each piece into a round about 1/8 inch thick. Fit two of the rounds into two 4-inch pie plates. Fill each with half of the cherry mixture; drape the remaining rounds over the pies and crimp the edges to seal. Cut slits into the tops of the pies for ventilation and bake until the filling is bubbling and crust is golden—50 to 60 minutes. Transfer to a wire rack to cool completely.

NUTRITION PER SERVING (SOUR-CHERRY PIE): calories: 508; protein: 5 g; fat: 21 g; carbohydrate: 79 g; fiber: 2.5 g; sodium: 143 mg; cholesterol: 54 mg

NUTRITION PER SERVING (SWEET-CHERRY PIE): calories: 410; protein: 5 g; fat: 21 g; carbohydrate: 62 g; fiber: 3 g; sodium: 140 mg; cholesterol: 54 mg

< **88** >

Classic Blueberry Pie

A homemade pie will take pride of place at any picnic. This irresistible blueberry pie—perfect for the Fourth of July—uses a mix of butter and vegetable shortening for the crust. Instead of venting the pie with slits, a decorative star shape is cut out of the top crust.

MAKES: ONE 10-INCH PIE (10 SERVINGS)

4 1/4 cups all-purpose flour

1 cup plus 2 tablespoons sugar

1/2 teaspoon salt

1 1/4 cups unsalted butter, chilled and cubed

1/4 cup vegetable shortening, chilled

1 teaspoon vinegar

3/4 cup ice water

3 pints fresh blueberries, stems removed

1/2 teaspoon freshly grated ginger

1/2 teaspoon lemon zest

1 tablespoon fresh lemon juice

1 tablespoon heavy cream

1. Combine the flour, 1/4 cup sugar, and salt in a large bowl. Cut in the butter and shortening using a pastry blender, 2 knives, or your fingers until the mixture resembles coarse meal. Add the vinegar and the water—sprinkling in a few tablespoons at a time as necessary (you may not need it all)—and mix until just combined. Gather the dough into a ball, divide it in two, and form each half into a disk. Wrap the disks tightly in plastic and chill for at least 1 hour or overnight.

2. Preheat the oven to 425°F. On a lightly floured surface, between two sheets of waxed paper, roll 1 pastry disk into a round at least 12 inches in diameter and 1/16 inch thick. Transfer the dough to a 10-inch pie plate and trim it, leaving a 1/2-inch overhang; fold the overhanging pastry under and pinch the dough to crimp it around the rim. Line the shell with parchment paper and fill with it dried beans or pie weights. Bake until lightly browned—about 10 minutes. Remove the beans and paper and

bake the shell for 10 minutes longer. Transfer to a wire rack to cool completely. Reduce the oven temperature to 400°F. Roll the second pastry disk to the same size as the first one, then place it on a baking sheet lined with waxed paper. Cover and refrigerate both parts of the crust.

3. Toss the blueberries with the ginger, lemon zest and juice, and $3/4$ cup sugar in a large bowl. Transfer the filling to the prepared crust. Using a small star-shaped cookie cutter, cut a ventilation hole in the center of the top crust, then drape the dough over the filling, taking care not to stretch the star hole out of shape; crimp the edges of the crust to seal them. Lightly brush the top crust with the cream and sprinkle on the remaining 2 tablespoons sugar. Loosely cover the crimped edge of the crust with strips of foil to prevent overbrowning. Bake the pie for 15 minutes, then reduce the oven temperature to 375°F and continue baking until the blueberry filling bubbles and crust is golden brown—about 45 minutes. Transfer to a wire rack to cool completely.

NUTRITION PER SERVING: calories: 630; protein: 7 g; fat: 39 g; carbohydrate: 67 g; fiber: 3 g; sodium: 115 mg; cholesterol: 75 mg

Nectarine-Blueberry Pie

This beautiful pie is filled with the tastes of summer. You'll feel like the ultimate host when you serve it at a picnic or barbecue.

MAKES: ONE 9-INCH PIE (10 SERVINGS)

1/2 **recipe (2 disks) Grandma's Pie Dough (page 85)**

3 1/2 **pounds nectarines, halved, pitted, and sliced** 1/2 **inch thick**

3/4 **cups fresh blueberries, stems removed**

3/4 **cup plus 1 tablespoon sugar**

3 **tablespoons quick-cooking tapioca, ground in a coffee mill or spice grinder**

2 **tablespoons fresh lemon juice**

1 **teaspoon finely grated lemon zest**

1 **large egg**

1 **tablespoon whole milk**

1. Preheat the oven to 450°F. On a lightly floured surface, roll the disks of dough into rounds about 1/8 inch thick; transfer one to a 9-inch pie pan. Place the remaining round on a baking sheet lined with parchment paper; chill both.

2. In a large bowl, toss together the nectarines, blueberries, 3/4 cup sugar, tapioca, lemon juice and zest. Set aside for 15 minutes, then drain through a fine-meshed sieve. In a small bowl, beat together the egg and milk; set aside.

3. Fill the prepared bottom crust with the fruit mixture, and top it with the second dough round. Seal and flute the edges; brush the top with some of the prepared egg wash.

4. Cut a few slits in the top crust. Bake the pie for 10 minutes, then reduce the oven temperature to 425°F. Continue baking the pie for 25 minutes, then brush it with the remaining egg wash, sprinkle it with the remaining 1 tablespoon sugar, and continue to bake until golden brown—about 5 minutes longer. Cool on a wire rack.

NUTRITION PER SERVING: calories: 415; protein: 5 g; fat: 17 g; carbohydrate: 61 g; fiber: 2 g; sodium: 105 mg; cholesterol: 82 mg

< 92 >

Cherry-Berry Lattice Pie

Since sweet cherries have a short season, they are a hallmark of summer. Here, we toss them with blueberries and encase the filling in a flaky latticework crust.

MAKES: ONE 10-INCH PIE (10 SERVINGS)

2 1/2 cups all-purpose flour

1/2 teaspoon salt

1/2 cup (1 stick) unsalted butter, chilled and cut into 2-inch pieces

1/2 cup vegetable shortening, chilled and cut into 1-inch pieces

1/3 cup ice water

4 cups (2 pints) fresh blueberries, stems removed

2 cups fresh sweet cherries, pitted

3/4 cup sugar

3 tablespoons quick-cooking tapioca

1. In a large bowl, combine the flour and salt. Using a pastry blender or large fork, cut in the butter until pea-size pieces remain. Add the shortening and cut it in until the mixture resembles coarse crumbs. Gradually add the water 1 tablespoon at a time, tossing with the fork until combined. Gather the dough together and divide it in half. Flatten each ball into a 6-inch disk; wrap it in plastic, and refrigerate at least 1 hour.

2. In a clean large bowl, combine the blueberries, cherries, sugar, and tapioca. Mix well and let the filling stand for 15 minutes. Preheat the oven to 400°F.

3. On a lightly floured surface, roll a piece of dough into an 11 1/2-inch round; fit it into a 10-inch pie pan. Roll the remaining dough into a round of the same size; cut it into 12 strips, each about 3/4 inch wide. Fill the pie pan with the fruit mixture. Weave the strips into a lattice pattern over the fruit as described on page 83. Trim the edges and pinch the top and bottom crusts together.

4. Bake the pie for 20 minutes, then reduce the heat to 375°F. Continue baking until the crust is golden and the filling is bubbly—30 to 40 minutes longer. (If necessary, cover the edges of the crust with strips of foil to prevent overbrowning.) Transfer to a wire rack to cool completely.

NUTRITION PER SERVING: calories: 400; protein: 4 g; fat: 20 g; carbohydrate: 52 g; fiber: 3 g; 189 mg: cholesterol: 25 mg sodium

Strawberry-Rhubarb Pie

Rhubarb and strawberries are a classic combination.
Encased in a golden-brown pie crust, the pairing becomes divine.

MAKES: ONE 9-INCH PIE (8 SERVINGS)

½ **recipe (2 disks) Grandma's Pie Dough (page 85)**

1⅓ **pounds rhubarb, trimmed and cut into 1-inch pieces (see Tip)**

⅓ **pound strawberries, hulled and halved**

¾ **cup sugar**

⅓ **cup all-purpose flour**

1. Preheat the oven to 375°F and position the rack in the center. On a lightly floured surface, roll a disk of dough into a round about ⅛ inch thick and transfer it to a 9-inch pie pan. Set aside and keep chilled. Roll the remaining dough to ⅛ inch thick. If you like, use a miniature star cutter (or other small shape) to create decorative vents in the top crust.

2. Combine the rhubarb, strawberries, sugar, and flour in a large bowl, then transfer the mixture to the prepared pie pan. Drape the rolled-out dough over the pie, taking care not to stretch the decorative vents out of shape. (If you did not cut decorative holes in the top crust, use a sharp paring knife to cut slits in it now.) Trim the edges of both crusts, leaving a ½-inch overhang. Fold the dough under and lightly pinch it to seal the top and bottom crusts. Crimp around the rim and chill for 10 minutes.

3. Bake until the crust is golden brown and the filling is bubbling— 45 to 55 minutes. Transfer to a wire rack to cool completely.

TIP: If you can't find fresh rhubarb, use frozen. You'll find it in the grocer's freezer section.

NUTRITION PER SERVING: calories: 410; protein: 5 g; fat: 21 g; carbohydrate: 53 g; fiber: 3 g; sodium: 121 mg; cholesterol: 68 mg

Blueberry-Peach Lattice Pie

Make the most of two beloved summer fruits—succulent blueberries and juicy, sweet peaches—by baking this luscious pie topped with a pretty lattice crust. For photo, see page 80.

MAKES: ONE 10-INCH PIE (10 SERVINGS)

CRUST

2 1/2 cups all-purpose flour

3/4 cup sugar

1/2 teaspoon salt

14 tablespoons unsalted butter, chilled and cut into small pieces

1/2 teaspoon pure vanilla extract

3 to 5 tablespoons ice water

FILLING

1 pint (2 cups) fresh blueberries, stems removed

3 cups peeled, sliced fresh peaches

3/4 cup plus 1 tablespoon sugar

3 tablespoons cornstarch

1/2 teaspoon ground cinnamon

1/2 teaspoon grated lemon zest

1 large egg, lightly beaten

1. **For the crust:** In a large bowl, combine the flour, sugar, and salt. Cut in the butter using a pastry blender, 2 knives, or your fingers until the mixture resembles coarse meal. Using a fork, mix in the vanilla, then add the water 1 tablespoon at a time just until the mixture begins to cling together. Gather the dough into a ball, divide it in half, and flatten each piece into a disk. Wrap the disks tightly in plastic and refrigerate for 1 hour or up to overnight.

2. Preheat the oven to 425°F and position the rack in the center. On a floured surface, roll 1 pastry disk into a round 12 inches in diameter. Transfer the dough round to a 10-inch pie pan. Trim the dough, leaving a 1/2-inch overhang. Fold the overhanging pastry under and pinch the dough to crimp it around the rim. Cut out a circle of parchment paper to cover the bottom of the dough and line it with pie weights or dried beans. Bake the shell for 10 minutes. Transfer to a wire rack and remove the weights and paper. Lower the oven temperature to 375°F.

3. Remove the remaining pastry disk from the refrigerator. On a floured surface, roll it into a thin circle. Use a pizza wheel or fluted pastry cutter to cut 10 strips, each about 1 inch wide. Transfer the strips to a parchment-lined baking sheet, cover them with plastic wrap, and chill until ready to use.

4. **Make the filling and assemble the pie:** In a large bowl, combine the blueberries and peaches. In a small bowl, combine $3/4$ cup sugar with the cornstarch, cinnamon, and lemon zest. Add the cornstarch mixture to the fruit and gently toss to coat. Pour the filling into the baked piecrust. Weave the reserved pastry strips into a lattice pattern over the fruit as described on page 83. Lightly brush the lattice with beaten egg and sprinkle with the remaining 1 tablespoon sugar.

5. Loosely cover the crimped edge of the crust with foil to prevent overbrowning. Bake the pie until the filling bubbles and the crust is golden brown—about 45 minutes. Transfer to a wire rack to cool completely.

NUTRITION PER SERVING: calories: 560; protein: 6 g; fat: 22 g; carbohydrate: 87 g; fiber: 3 g; sodium: 172 mg; cholesterol: 77 mg

Peach-Huckleberry Lattice Pie

This lovely lattice crust creates a patchwork of colors and textures,
a pleasing pattern of baked fruit peeking from beneath strips
of tender pastry. Huckleberries are wild, blue-black berries
that resemble blueberries, but are more tart in flavor.
They are in season from June through August.

MAKES: ONE 9-INCH PIE (8 SERVINGS)

$\frac{1}{2}$ **recipe (2 disks)
Grandma's Pie Dough
(page 85)**

**5 cups 1-inch peach slices
(from about 5 medium
peaches)**

$\frac{1}{2}$ **cup fresh huckleberries**

$\frac{3}{4}$ **cup sugar**

$\frac{1}{4}$ **cup all-purpose flour**

$\frac{1}{2}$ **teaspoon ground
cinnamon**

1. Preheat the oven to 400°F. On a lightly floured surface, roll a disk of dough into a round about $\frac{1}{8}$ inch thick. Transfer it to a 9-inch pie pan and trim the edges, leaving a $\frac{1}{2}$-inch overhang. Set the shell aside and keep it chilled. Roll the remaining disk of dough into a round the same size as the first. Cut ten 1-inch strips using a pizza wheel or fluted pastry cutter. Lay the strips on a parchment paper–lined baking sheet, cover them with plastic wrap, and chill until ready to use.

2. Toss the peaches, huckleberries, sugar, flour, and cinnamon together in a large bowl. Pour the filling into the prepared pie shell. Weave the pastry strips into a lattice pattern over the fruit as described on page 83. Chill the pie for 10 minutes, then bake it until the fruit is bubbling and the crust is golden brown—50 to 55 minutes. Transfer to a wire rack to cool completely.

NUTRITION PER SERVING: calories: 432; protein: 5 g; fat: 21 g; carbohydrate: 59 g; fiber: 2 g; sodium: 118 mg; cholesterol: 68 mg

Shaker Lemon Pie

This sweet yet citrusy pie owes a debt of gratitude to Shaker settlers of the early nineteenth century who had the brilliant idea of filling a tender crust with thinly sliced lemons marinated in sugar. This rendition comes from the Golden Lamb, an inn and restaurant in Lebanon, Ohio, since 1803. The lemon slices must macerate in the sugar overnight, so plan ahead.

MAKES: ONE 9-INCH PIE (8 SERVINGS)

2 large lemons, sliced very thin

2 cups sugar

5 large eggs, beaten

2 (9-inch) store-bought unroll-and-fill piecrusts

1. In a medium-size, nonreactive bowl, mix together the lemon slices and sugar; cover and let them stand in the refrigerator overnight. Before proceeding, allow the lemon slices to return to room temperature. Preheat the oven to 350°F.

2. Fit a crust into a 9-inch pie pan. Stir the eggs into the lemon mixture and pour the filling into the pie pan. Top with the remaining crust. Trim the excess dough, fold the top crust under the bottom all around, and crimp to seal the edges. Bake until the crust is golden-brown—about 45 minutes. Transfer to a wire rack to cool completely.

NUTRITION PER SERVING: calories: 470; protein: 6 g; fat: 17 g; carbohydrate: 79 g; fiber: 2 g; sodium: 326 mg; cholesterol: 138 mg

Quince Mince Pie

Mincemeat, quince, and Granny Smith apples make this pie
as delightfully golden as the childhood memories we associate
with it. For a decorative flourish, it is finished with
ornamental cutouts instead of a top crust. To save time,
the recipe calls for store-bought pie dough.

MAKES: ONE 9-INCH PIE (8 SERVINGS)

1 tablespoon finely chopped
crystallized ginger

1 tablespoon sugar

2 cups store-bought mincemeat
filling

1/4 cup brandy

2 Granny Smith apples, peeled
and finely chopped

2 quinces, peeled and finely
chopped

1 cup chopped walnuts

1 cup golden raisins

Juice and zest of 2 oranges

Juice and zest of 1 lemon

2 (9-inch) store-bought unroll-
and-fill piecrusts

2 teaspoons water

1 large egg, beaten

1. In a small food processor, combine the crystallized ginger and
sugar. Process until the mixture is finely chopped; set aside. Place
the mincemeat, brandy, apples, quinces, walnuts, raisins, and
orange zest and juice in a large saucepan and bring the mixture to a
simmer. Continue to cook over medium-low heat, covered, until the
fruit is tender—about 30 minutes. Stir in the lemon zest and juice.
Let the filling cool to room temperature. Preheat the oven to 375°F.

2. Fit one of the dough rounds into a 9-inch pie pan. Pour in the filling. Use small decorative cookie cutters to make cutout patterns in the remaining dough round and set the cutouts aside. Place the round carefully over the pie, taking care not to stretch the holes out of shape, and crimp the edges to seal. Add the water to the egg to make a wash and brush the edges of the crust and the surface with it. Sprinkle the pie with some of the reserved ginger-sugar mixture.

3. Transfer the reserved cutout crust pieces to a cookie sheet, brush them with the egg wash, and sprinkle them with the remaining ginger sugar. Bake the cutouts until they are just golden—about 12 minutes. Set them on a wire rack to cool.

4. Bake the pie until the top is golden and the filling is bubbling—35 to 45 minutes. Decorate the pie with the cutout pastry pieces. Transfer to a wire rack to cool. Serve warm.

NUTRITION PER SERVING: calories: 1,075; protein: 11 g; fat: 58 g; carbohydrate: 126 g; fiber: 5 g; sodium: 308 mg; cholesterol: 120 mg

elegant
tarts & tartlets

A TART FOR EVERY OCCASION

If you always wondered about the differences between a tart and a pie, the distinction lies not in the filling, topping, or pan, but in the crust. A dessert tart crust is sweet, buttery, and crumbly, like a shortbread cookie. It should taste good enough on its own to satisfy a sweet tooth—and the recipes that follow do! A piecrust, on the other hand, is savory and has a crisp, flaky texture; the sweetness of a dessert pie comes from the filling.

In this chapter, we provide a sampling of both sweet and savory tarts of various sizes, shapes, and flavors to serve as appetizers, main courses, or desserts. The savory tart crusts are scented with fresh herbs—from thyme to rosemary—so they, too, are flavorful enough to nibble minus the filling!

You will come across tart pans in a wide range of sizes—for making one- or two-bite hors d'oeuvres to individual-serving-size tartlets to full-size tarts to feed a crowd. They also come in squares and rectangles, as well as the traditional rounds. Tart pans are shallower than pie plates and typically feature fluted edges. To show off these golden-brown decorative edges to full effect, select a pan with a removable bottom, which will allow you to unmold the finished tart with ease. If you enjoy making tarts, you'll soon find yourself with a collection of various sizes and shapes of pans (check flea markets and tag sales for steals). But if you are just beginning, start out with a 9-inch round pan—that's the most common and versatile shape.

Although the ingredients of the dough are different, the instructions for rolling and shaping a tart or tartlet are approximately the same as for a single-crust pie (see page 17). For tarts, there's no need for decorative pinching around the rim, though, because the fluted edges do that automatically—just gently press the dough into the mold and trim it even around the rim (see page 19 for tips). Depending on the type of filling, a tart shell can be baked and then filled, or filled and then baked. Follow recipe instructions.

Sweet Pastry Crust

This classic crust is perfect for a wide variety of sweet tarts.
Try it in the Rosemary Strawberry Tart on page 112
or the Raspberry Fig Tart on page 116.

★ **MAKES ONE 9-INCH TART SHELL (8 SERVINGS)** ★

1¼ **cups all-purpose flour**

3 **tablespoons sugar**

⅛ **teaspoon salt**

½ **cup (1 stick cold butter), cut into small pieces**

1 **large egg yolk**

2 **tablespoons ice water**

1. In a large bowl, stir together flour and sugar. Cut the butter with a pastry blender, 2 knives, or your fingers until the mixture resembles coarse meal. In a small bowl, beat together the egg yolk and ice water. Add it to the flour mixture, tossing lightly with a fork until the dough is moist enough to hold together when lightly pressed. Shape the dough into a ball and flatten into a disk, wrap it in plastic, and refrigerate for at least 1 hour or overnight.

2. Place the disk between 2 sheets of floured waxed paper and roll the dough out to an 11-inch round. Remove the top sheet of waxed paper and invert the dough into a 9-inch fluted tart pan with a removable bottom, gently pressing the dough into the bottom and up sides of the pan. Peel off the remaining sheet of waxed paper. If the dough cracks, gently press it together. Run a rolling pin over the top of the pan to trim off excess dough. With a fork, pierce the bottom of the crust. Refrigerate until chilled—10 to 15 minutes. Prebake the crust or fill and bake according to recipe instructions.

NUTRITION PER ⅛ RECIPE: calories: 200; protein: 3 g; fat: 12 g; carbohydrate: 20g; fiber: 1 g; sodium: 155 mg; cholesterol: 58 mg

Chocolate-Pecan Tartlets

These tarts are sweet and oh so rich, but worth the splurge
for special occasions. Come Kentucky Derby time, revelers
beat a path to Sweet Surrender Dessert Café for these buttery,
miniature takes on the classic chocolate-pecan pie known as
Derby Pie. For a little extra kick, owner Jessica Haskell advises
soaking the pecans in bourbon the night before you bake
the tartlets. You'll need ten 3½-inch tartlet pans.

MAKES: 10 TARTLETS

CRUST

2 cups (4 sticks) unsalted butter, chilled and cut into 1/2-inch cubes, plus more for greasing pans

5 cups all-purpose flour

1 cup ice water

FILLING

8 ounces pecan halves

1 cup sugar

1 tablespoon all-purpose flour

4 large eggs

1 cup light corn syrup

1 tablespoon unsalted butter, melted

2/3 cup semisweet chocolate chips

1. **For the crust:** Butter ten 3 1/2-inch tartlet pans; set aside. In a medium-size bowl, cut the butter into the flour using a pastry cutter, 2 knives, or your fingers until the mixture resembles coarse meal with bean-size bits mixed in. Slowly drizzle in the ice water and mix just until dough forms—you may not need all the water. Do not overwork.

2. On a lightly floured surface, roll out half the dough 1/8 inch thick. With a sharp knife, cut five 6-inch circles and fit them into the prepared pans. Trim the excess dough from the rims, saving the scraps. Repeat the process with the remaining half of the dough. Gather and reroll the scraps as needed. Place the tartlet pans on 2 baking sheets; set aside. Preheat the oven to 325°F.

3. **For the filling:** Chop enough of the pecans to make 2/3 cup and set nearby; reserve the remaining pecan halves. In a large bowl, mix together the sugar and flour. Whisk in the eggs, corn syrup, and butter until combined. Mix in the chopped pecans and the chocolate chips. Divide the mixture evenly among the prepared tartlet pans. Arrange the pecan halves on top of the filling.

4. Bake until golden on the edges and set in the center—about 25 minutes. Transfer to a wire rack to cool completely, then chill overnight so that the tartlets fully set.

NUTRITION PER SERVING: calories: 979; protein: 12 g; fat: 60 g; carbohydrate: 106 g; fiber: 5 g; sodium: 58 mg; cholesterol: 185 mg

< 111 >

Rosemary Strawberry Tart

Zip up a classic strawberry tart with a faint, aniselike perfume by adding tarragon to the crust and tarragon and rosemary to the syrup. Other berries to try: raspberries and blackberries, alone or in combination. Don't forget to plan ahead for draining the yogurt. This takes at least four hours but is well worth it—the yogurt becomes luxuriously dense and creamy. You will need a 9-inch fluted tart pan.

MAKES: ONE 9-INCH TART (8 SERVINGS)

3 cups vanilla-flavored yogurt

1½ cups all-purpose flour

1 cup sugar

3 tablespoons chopped fresh tarragon leaves, plus a sprig for garnish

¼ teaspoon baking powder

¼ teaspoon salt

½ cup (1 stick) butter, cut into chunks

1 large egg

1 large egg yolk

½ cup water

1 tablespoon chopped fresh rosemary leaves

1 tablespoon fresh lemon juice

2 pints fresh strawberries, hulled

1. Place the yogurt in a strainer lined with a large coffee filter; set it over a bowl. Let it drain, covered, in the refrigerator for 4 hours or up to overnight.

2. In a medium-size bowl, combine the flour, ¼ cup sugar, 1 tablespoon chopped tarragon, baking powder, and salt. Cut in the butter using a pastry blender, 2 knives, or your fingers until the mixture resembles coarse meal.

3. In a small bowl, beat the egg and egg yolk. Add it to the flour mixture, tossing lightly with a fork until the dough is moist enough to hold together when lightly pressed. Shape the dough into a ball and flatten it into a disk, wrap it in plastic, and refrigerate for at least 1 hour.

< 112 >

4. Meanwhile, in a 1-quart saucepan over medium-high heat, combine the water, remaining $^3/_4$ cup sugar, remaining 2 tablespoons tarragon, and the rosemary. Heat to boiling, then reduce the heat to low and cook until thickened—7 to 10 minutes. Remove the pan from the heat and stir in the lemon juice. Let cool completely.

5. Preheat the oven to 375°F. Between 2 sheets of floured waxed paper, roll the dough out to an 11-inch round. Remove the top sheet of waxed paper and invert the dough into a 9-inch tart pan with a removable bottom.

6. Peel off the remaining sheet of waxed paper and fold the edge of the dough to fit into the pan. With a fork, pierce the bottom of the crust. Bake until the edges are lightly browned and the bottom is firm to the touch—12 to 15 minutes. Transfer to a wire rack to cool completely.

7. To assemble the tart, remove the rim of the pan. Evenly spread the thickened yogurt over the bottom of the crust. Place the strawberries, cut side down, in a decorative pattern on top of the yogurt. Brush the strawberries with the herb syrup and pour the remaining syrup into a pitcher to make available while serving. Garnish the tart with the tarragon sprig.

NUTRITION PER SERVING: calories: 382; protein: 8 g; fat: 14 g; carbohydrate: 57 g; fiber: 2 g; sodium: 241 mg; cholesterol: 87 mg

Key Lime Tart

Louie's Backyard in Key West, Florida, bakes up this creamy variation on Key lime pie. Instead of the familiar graham-cracker crust, they use a ginger-molasses pastry that contrasts beautifully with the zestiness of the limes.

MAKES: ONE 11-INCH TART (8 SERVINGS)

CRUST

1/3 cup sugar

1/2 cup (1 stick) unsalted butter, at room temperature

1 pinch salt

1 1/2 cups plus 2 tablespoons all-purpose flour

1 large egg

1/2 teaspoon pure vanilla extract

2 tablespoons molasses

1/2 tablespoon ground ginger

1/4 teaspoon ground cinnamon

FILLING

1 (14-ounce) can sweetened condensed milk

1/2 cup Key lime juice

4 large egg yolks

1 tablespoon vanilla extract

1. **For the crust:** Preheat the oven to 325°F. In a medium-size bowl, cream the sugar, butter, and salt until smooth. Add the flour, egg, vanilla, molasses, ginger, and cinnamon and mix well to form a smooth dough. On a lightly floured surface, roll the dough into a 13-inch round about 1/4 inch thick. Gently press the dough into an 11-inch tart pan with a removable bottom. Trim the excess around the rim. Bake until browned—12 to 15 minutes.

2. **Assemble the tart:** In a medium-size bowl, whisk together all the filling ingredients. Pour the mixture into the prepared shell and bake until the filling sets to the consistency of a soft custard—about 15 minutes. Transfer to a wire rack to cool completely.

NUTRITION PER SERVING: calories: 450; protein: 9 g; fat: 19 g; carbohydrate: 60 g; fiber: 1 g; sodium: 99 mg; cholesterol: 195 mg

< 114 >

Raspberry and Fig Tart

The sublime flavor of fresh figs plays off the tang of red raspberries
in this sophisticated almond-crust tart. In order to display
the golden-brown fluted edge of the crust, you will need an 9½-inch
tart pan with a removable bottom. For photo, see page 106.

MAKES: ONE 9 ½-INCH TART (8 SERVINGS)

ALMOND CRUST

1 cup unsifted all-purpose flour

½ cup ground natural almonds

2 tablespoons sugar

¼ teaspoon salt

½ cup (1 stick) unsalted butter, chilled and cut into small pieces

1 teaspoon almond extract

2 to 4 tablespoons ice water

FILLING

⅓ cup seedless red-raspberry preserves

2 tablespoons fresh lemon juice

6 large fresh figs (about 8 ounces)

1 cup (½ pint) fresh red raspberries

Fresh mint sprigs (optional)

1. **For the almond crust:** In a medium-size bowl, combine the flour, almonds, sugar, and salt. Cut in the butter using a pastry blender, 2 knives, or your fingers until the mixture resembles coarse meal. Sprinkle in the almond extract; add the ice water, 1 tablespoon at a time, tossing lightly with a fork until the pastry is moist enough to hold together when lightly pressed. Shape the pastry into a disk. Wrap it in plastic and refrigerate for 30 minutes. Preheat the oven to 375°F.

2. Between 2 sheets of floured waxed paper, roll the chilled pastry into a 12-inch round. Remove the top sheet of waxed paper and invert the pastry into a 9½-inch tart pan with a removable bottom, allowing the excess to extend over the edge. Peel off the remaining sheet of waxed paper. Fold the excess pastry inward so that the crust is even with the rim of the pan. Press the pastry against the sides to make an even thickness. With a fork, pierce the bottom of the pastry crust to prevent shrinkage and bubbling. Line the crust with a piece of aluminum foil, allowing it to extend over the edge of the crust, and fill it with pie weights or dried beans.

3. Bake the crust for 10 minutes, then remove the foil with the beans and bake until crisp and golden—12 to 15 minutes. Transfer to a wire rack to cool completely.

4. **Prepare the filling:** No more than 1 hour before serving, combine the preserves and lemon juice in a small bowl; set aside. Cut the figs lengthwise in half. With a pastry brush, spread 2 tablespoons of the preserve mixture evenly over the bottom of the crust. Arrange 8 fig halves, cut sides up, around the edge of the crust with the stems toward the center. Place the remaining 4 fig halves in the center with the stems pointing out.

5. Place 3 large berries in the center of the tart. Arrange the remaining berries in the spaces between the figs. Brush the remaining preserve mixture over the figs and berries.

6. Remove the rim of the pan from the tart. Place the tart on a serving plate and garnish with mint sprigs, if desired.

NUTRITION PER SERVING: calories: 270; protein: 3 g; fat: 15 g; carbohydrate: 33g; fiber: 3 g; sodium: 75 mg; cholesterol: 31 mg

Double Lemon Tart

This pretty tart can be made ahead of time and chilled, then caramelized under a broiler just before serving. Scented with rosemary, the filling contains lemon slices and lemon juice for double the lemon. You will need an 11-inch tart pan.

MAKES: ONE 11-INCH TART (12 SERVINGS)

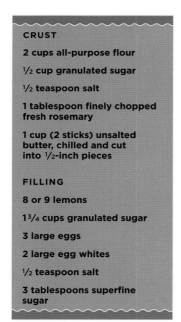

CRUST

2 cups all-purpose flour

1/2 cup granulated sugar

1/2 teaspoon salt

1 tablespoon finely chopped fresh rosemary

1 cup (2 sticks) unsalted butter, chilled and cut into 1/2-inch pieces

FILLING

8 or 9 lemons

1 3/4 cups granulated sugar

3 large eggs

2 large egg whites

1/2 teaspoon salt

3 tablespoons superfine sugar

1. **For the crust:** Preheat the oven to 350°F. In a food processor fitted with a metal blade, combine the flour, sugar, salt, and rosemary. Add the butter and pulse until the mixture resembles coarse meal. Or, to mix the crust by hand, combine the dry ingredients in a bowl and cut in the butter using a pastry blender, 2 knives, or your fingers. Transfer the mixture to an 11-inch tart pan; press it into the bottom and up along the side. Bake the crust until it is golden brown at the edges—15 to 20 minutes. Transfer to a wire rack to cool for about 15 minutes. Leave the oven on.

2. **For the filling:** Cut one of the lemons into very thin rounds; set aside. Using the remaining lemons, cut enough lemon sections to make 1 cup and squeeze 1/4 cup juice.

3. In a nonreactive pan over medium heat, combine the lemon sections, juice, and sugar. Cook, stirring occasionally, just until the sugar dissolves. In a medium-size bowl, lightly whisk the eggs, egg whites, and salt. While continually stirring, slowly pour the lemon mixture into the eggs. Pour the filling into the cooled crust, arrange the lemon slices on top, and bake the tart on the middle rack of the oven until the custard is set—about 30 minutes. If the edges begin to overbrown, cover the crust with strips of foil. Transfer to a wire rack to cool, then cover and refrigerate until completely chilled.

4. **Caramelize the tart:** Just before serving, position a rack in the uppermost part of the oven and heat the broiler. Sprinkle the superfine sugar over the chilled tart and place it under the broiler. Watching the tart closely as the sugar begins to bubble, carefully rotate it to ensure even browning. Remove the tart as soon as the sugar turns a golden-brown color—2 to 3 minutes. Serve immediately.

NUTRITION PER SERVING: calories: 430; protein: 7 g; fat: 25 g; carbohydrate: 46 g; fiber: 2 g; sodium: 309 mg; cholesterol: 142 mg

< 119 >

Tomato and Camembert Tart

In this showstopping tart, flaky pastry crust plays host to Gruyère and Camembert cheeses, sliced plum tomatoes, and a fragrant herb oil. You will need an 11-inch tart pan.

MAKES: ONE 11-INCH TART (12 SERVINGS)

- 1½ cups all-purpose flour

- 6 tablespoons unsalted butter, chilled and cut into ½-inch pieces

- ½ teaspoon salt

- ½ teaspoon coarsely ground black pepper

- 2 to 3 tablespoons plus ½ cup extra-virgin olive oil

- 1 tablespoon water

- 1 tablespoon Dijon mustard

- ½ cups grated Gruyère cheese

- 4 plum tomatoes, cut into ½-inch slices, seeds removed

- 6 ounces Camembert cheese, cut into ⅛-inch strips

- ¼ cup fresh parsley, chopped

- ¼ cup fresh basil, chopped

- 1 teaspoon fresh rosemary, finely chopped

- 1 tablespoon fresh thyme leaves

- 1 small bay leaf, finely crumbled

- 1 clove garlic, minced

1. Combine the flour, salt, and pepper and cut in the butter using a pastry blender, 2 knives, or your fingers until the mixture resembles coarse meal. Using a fork, mix in 2 tablespoons of the oil and the water, tossing just until the mixture begins to cling together. If necessary, add an additional tablespoon oil. Form the dough into a disk, wrap it in plastic, and chill for 30 minutes.

2. Preheat the oven to 375°F and place the rack in the middle position. On a lightly floured surface, roll the chilled dough into a 14-inch circle and fit it into an 11-inch tart pan with a removable bottom.

3. Spread the mustard over the bottom of the tart shell. Sprinkle the Gruyère evenly over the mustard and arrange the tomato and Camembert slices in alternation over the Gruyère.

4. In a small bowl, mix the remaining ½ cup olive oil, all the herbs, and the garlic and brush two-thirds of the mixture over the tart. Bake for 35 minutes. Brush the tart with the remaining herb oil; transfer to a wire rack to cool slightly before removing the rim from the tart pan. Serve warm.

NUTRITION PER SERVING: calories: 275; protein: 6 g; fat: 22 g; carbohydrate: 14 g; fiber: 1 g; sodium: 259 mg; cholesterol: 31 mg

Wild Mushroom Tart

This flavorful savory tart makes a satisfying supper. Serve it at room temperature alongside a simple green salad tossed in vinaigrette.

MAKES: ONE 9-INCH TART (6 SERVINGS)

CRUST

1 1/2 cups all-purpose flour

1/2 teaspoon salt

1/2 cup (1 stick) butter, chilled and cut into small pieces

2 to 3 tablespoons ice water

FILLING

1 cup unfiltered apple cider

3/4 cup dried porcini mushrooms

3 tablespoons olive oil

1/3 cup chopped shallots

8 ounces white mushrooms, sliced

4 ounces wild mushrooms (such as cremini, shiitake, or chanterelle), sliced

1/4 cup Calvados, applejack, or hard cider

1/2 cup chopped fresh flat-leaf parsley

1/2 teaspoon salt

1/4 teaspoon ground black pepper

4 large eggs

3/4 cup heavy cream

1 cup grated smoked mozzarella or smoked Gouda

1/2 cup grated Parmesan cheese

1. For the crust: In a food processor fitted with a metal blade, combine the flour, salt, and butter. Pulse until the mixture resembles coarse meal—about 6 pulses. With the processor running, add the ice water, 1 tablespoon at a time, just until the dough comes together, no longer than 15 seconds. Gather the dough into a rough ball, flatten it into a 7-inch disk, and wrap it in plastic. Refrigerate for at least 1 hour or up to 24 hours. Preheat the oven to 375°F.

< 122 >

2. Roll out the dough between 2 sheets of plastic wrap to an 11-inch round. Remove the top sheet of plastic wrap and invert the round into a 9-inch tart pan with a removable bottom. Carefully peel off the remaining sheet of plastic wrap. Tuck the dough into the pan and trim the edges so they are even with the top of the pan. Freeze the shell for 10 minutes. Line the bottom

of the prepared pan with waxed paper or foil and fill it with pie weights or dried beans. Bake for 20 minutes. Transfer to a wire rack to cool and remove the weights and paper. Leave the oven on.

3. **For the filling:** In a small saucepan or microwaveable container, bring the cider to a boil. Pour the hot liquid over the dried porcini mushrooms and let them hydrate for 10 minutes.

4. Heat the oil in a large skillet and sauté the shallots and all the fresh mushrooms for about 10 minutes. Add the hydrated porcini mushrooms, along with their soaking liquid, and the Calvados. Cook over medium-low heat until almost all the liquid is absorbed—about 15 minutes. Stir in the parsley, salt, and pepper.

5. In a large bowl, combine the eggs, cream, and cheeses. Stir in the mushroom mixture. Pour the filling into the prepared crust.

6. Bake the tart until a toothpick inserted in the center comes out clean and the top has browned—30 to 35 minutes. Transfer to a wire rack to cool slightly before removing the rim from the tart pan. Serve warm. (The tart may be prepared 1 day ahead and refrigerated. Reheat it in a 350°F oven for 20 to 25 minutes.)

NUTRITION PER SERVING: calories: 710; protein: 25 g; fat: 45 g; carbohydrate: 48 g; fiber: 7 g; sodium: 654 mg; cholesterol: 245 mg

Turkey and Autumn Vegetable Tart

A medley of fall flavors, this hearty supper tart puts your leftover Thanksgiving Day turkey to delicious use. At other times of year, use precooked dark-meat turkey from the supermarket.

MAKES: ONE 10-INCH TART (8 SERVINGS)

CRUST

1 1/2 cups unsifted all-purpose flour

1 teaspoon fresh thyme leaves

1/2 teaspoon salt

1/2 cup vegetable shortening, chilled

4 to 5 tablespoons ice water

FILLING

1 large (3/4-pound) sweet potato, peeled and cut into 1-inch cubes

1 (10-ounce) package thawed frozen Brussels sprouts

2 cups 1-inch pieces cooked turkey

4 tablespoons (1/2 stick) unsalted butter

1 medium onion, chopped

2 tablespoons all-purpose flour

2/3 cup turkey or chicken broth

2/3 cup whole milk

1/4 teaspoon salt

1/3 cup dried unseasoned bread crumbs

1/4 teaspoon fresh thyme leaves

1. **For the thyme crust:** In a medium-size bowl, combine the flour, thyme, and salt. Cut in the shortening using a pastry blender, 2 knives, or your fingers until the mixture resembles very coarse meal. Add the ice water, 1 tablespoon at a time, tossing with a fork until the mixture holds together when lightly pressed. Shape into a disk, wrap in waxed paper, and refrigerate until chilled—about 30 minutes.

2. Preheat the oven to 400°F. Roll the dough between 2 sheets of floured waxed paper into a 12-inch round. Remove the top sheet of waxed paper and invert the pastry into a 10-inch tart pan with removable bottom, allowing the excess to extend over the edge. Peel off the remaining sheet of waxed paper. Fold the excess pastry inside so that it is even with the rim of the pan; press the pastry against the side to an even thickness. With a fork, pierce the bottom of the pastry 10 to 12 times to prevent shrinkage during baking. Line the pastry with foil and fill with pie weights or dried beans. Bake the pastry for 15 minutes, then remove the foil and beans. Bake for 10 to 15 minutes longer, or until the bottom of the pastry is golden and crisp. Transfer to a wire rack to cool completely.

3. **Meanwhile, prepare the filling:** In a heavy 2-quart saucepan, combine the sweet potato with enough water to cover. Heat it to boiling over high heat. Reduce the heat to low; cover and cook for 10 minutes. Add the Brussels sprouts and cook for 5 minutes longer. Drain well and transfer to a bowl. Fold the turkey into the sweet potatoes and Brussels sprouts; set aside.

4. Wipe out the saucepan and melt the butter in it. Set aside 2 tablespoons of the melted butter in a small bowl. Add the onion to the butter remaining in the saucepan and sauté until golden. Stir in the flour until completely incorporated. Gradually stir in the broth, milk, and salt. Heat to boiling, stirring constantly, until the sauce thickens.

5. **Assemble and bake the tart:** Fold $1/2$ cup sauce into the turkey and vegetable mixture. Spoon the filling into the pastry shell and top it with the remaining sauce. Combine the reserved melted butter with the bread crumbs and thyme. Sprinkle the crumb mixture over the filling. Bake the tart until the crumbs brown—8 to 10 minutes. Transfer to a wire rack to cool slightly before removing the rim of the pan. Serve warm.

NUTRITION PER SERVING: calories: 400; protein: 16 g; fat: 22 g; carbohydrate: 35 g; fiber: 3 g; sodium: 414 mg; cholesterol: 45 mg

hand pies & turnovers

PIES THAT SERVE ONE

This chapter is bursting with treats we like to call "hand pies" (although you may be more familiar with the older, and still-popular, term "turnovers"). These single-serving pockets of pastry can have a sweet or savory filling tucked inside. Hand pies can be folded to create rectangles, half moons, or triangles. The edges may be rustically crimped or pinched into repeating patterns for a fancier look. They range from bite-size to about six inches long. Because they are packaged as individual servings, hand pies are an obvious choice for appetizers. They also make pretty desserts that you don't have to feel compelled to share!

These pastries may be baked or deep-fried, like our Fried Apricot Turnovers (page 132). The recipes in this chapter make use of a variety of pie doughs—store-bought for ease or delectably homemade, as well as flaky phyllo. The ones made from pie dough are an excellent choice

for anyone who thinks the crust is the best part of a wedge of pie—they have an even higher proportion of yummy golden pastry to filling. The edges of pie dough turnovers are typically crimped or pinched to prevent the filling from leaking. This is not possible with phyllo dough, however, so it is best folded into triangles, which help keep the filling inside where it belongs.

The chapter closes with a recipe for empanadas, a traditional Latin American style of turnover featuring a pastry crust and usually filled with a savory meat mixture. But why not fill them with fruit and serve them for dessert? You could also stuff them with ingredients from other cultures. Our Quiche Lorraine Empanadas (page 138) offer a traditional French filling in a thoroughly Latin American presentation.

Cream Cheese and Jelly Turnovers

Shaped from store-bought dough and stuffed with a sweet, creamy filling, these turnovers will appeal to both kids and adults.

MAKES: 8 TURNOVERS

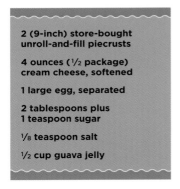

2 (9-inch) store-bought unroll-and-fill piecrusts

4 ounces (½ package) cream cheese, softened

1 large egg, separated

2 tablespoons plus 1 teaspoon sugar

⅛ teaspoon salt

½ cup guava jelly

1. Preheat the oven to 450°F. Line 2 baking pans with parchment paper. Unroll each piecrust round and cut it into quarters. Carefully fold each dough piece in half lengthwise, creating a crease, and open it again so that it lies flat. On each dough piece, cut four horizontal ventilation slits to one side of the crease, leaving a ½-inch border of uncut dough along the outer edge of that side.

2. Place the cream cheese, egg yolk, 1 tablespoon sugar, and salt in a small bowl and stir until combined and smooth. Place a generous 1 tablespoon of the cream cheese mixture onto the uncut side of each dough triangle. Spread it out slightly, leaving a ½-inch border. Spread 1 tablespoon jelly on top of the cheese layer. Lightly brush egg white around the edges of the dough. Fold the cut side over the filled side and crimp the edges with a fork.

3. Place turnovers on the prepared baking pans. Lightly brush them with egg white and sprinkle each with ½ teaspoon sugar. Bake until the pastry is golden brown—12 to 14 minutes. Serve warm.

NUTRITION PER TURNOVER: calories: 500; protein: 7 g; fat: 30; carbohydrate: 50 g; fiber: 1.5 g; sodium: 478 mg; cholesterol: 43 mg

Apple Butter and Oatmeal Breakfast Pockets

For a morning meal on the go, pack one of these wholesome
hand pies. The oatmeal and wheat germ crust enfolds
an apple butter filling.

MAKES: 8 TURNOVERS

1 ³/₄ cups all-purpose flour

1 ¹/₄ cups quick-cooking rolled oats

¹/₂ cup wheat germ

1 teaspoon baking powder

¹/₂ teaspoon ground cinnamon

¹/₄ teaspoon salt

¹/₈ teaspoon ground nutmeg

1 cup (2 sticks) unsalted butter

¹/₂ cup plus 2 tablespoons light brown sugar

2 large eggs

1 teaspoon pure vanilla extract

1 cup apple butter

1. Combine the flour, oats, wheat germ, baking powder, cinnamon, salt, and nutmeg in a medium bowl. Using an electric mixer set on high speed, beat the butter and sugar until light and fluffy. Add the eggs, one at a time, blending thoroughly after each addition. Add the vanilla. Reduce the speed to low. Stir in the flour mixture. Divide the dough in half, wrap it in plastic, and chill for 1 hour.

2. Roll out a piece of the dough between two sheets of lightly floured parchment paper into an 8-by-10-inch rectangle about ¹/₈ inch thick. Cut each dough piece into quarters, making eight 2-by-5-inch rectangles of dough. Repeat with the second half of the dough.

3. Place about 2 tablespoons apple butter along the center of a piece of dough, top it with another piece of dough, and crimp the edges with a fork. Transfer the turnovers to a parchment-lined baking sheet, cover them with plastic wrap, and chill for 20 minutes while you preheat the oven to 375°F.

4. Bake the pockets until they are lightly golden—20 to 25 minutes. Transfer to a wire rack to cool completely.

NUTRITION PER TURNOVER: calories: 478; protein: 8 g; fat: 26 g; carbohydrate: 55 g; fiber: 4 g; sodium: 139 mg; cholesterol: 115 mg

Fried Apricot Turnovers

These delectable little pies are filled with fresh, ripe apricots,
then deep-fried into individual desserts cloaked in crusts so
gloriously flaky they'll put ordinary baked pies to the test.
Before wrapping the fruit in the dough, taste it to assess sweetness,
and add some sugar or honey if necessary.

MAKES: 10 TURNOVERS

- 2 cups all-purpose flour

- 1 1/2 tablespoons granulated sugar

- 1 teaspoon baking powder

- 1/2 teaspoon salt

- 1/2 cup (1 stick) unsalted butter, chilled and cubed

- 2 tablespoons vegetable shortening, chilled

- 6 to 8 tablespoons ice water

- 1/3 cup ginger marmalade

- 5 small ripe apricots (2 ounces each), halved and pitted

- 2 teaspoons ground nutmeg (optional)

- 3 cups canola oil

- 1/4 cup confectioners' sugar, for dusting

1. Combine the flour, granulated sugar, baking powder, and salt in a medium bowl. Cut in the butter and shortening using a pastry blender, 2 knives, or your fingers until the mixture resembles coarse meal. Add the ice water, 1 tablespoon at a time, tossing with a fork, stopping as soon as a dough forms. Gather the dough into a ball and divide it into 10 equal pieces. Slightly flatten each piece into a disk and wrap in plastic. Chill for 1 hour.

2. On a lightly floured surface, roll a dough disk into a thin 5-inch round. Spoon 1 teaspoon ginger marmalade into the pit hollow of an apricot half and place it, cut side down, on the lower third of the pastry round. Sprinkle it with nutmeg, if desired. Lightly brush the edge of the dough with cold water and fold it over the apricot. Pinch the edges together to seal and trim away any overlapping dough. Crimp the edge with the floured tines of a fork on both sides. Repeat for the remaining dough disks and apricot halves.

3. Heat the oil over medium-high heat in a 4-quart Dutch oven fitted with a deep-fat thermometer. When the oil reaches 360°F, fry the turnovers, 2 at a time, until they are golden brown—4 to 5 minutes. Using a slotted spoon, transfer them to a wire rack to drain. Let the turnovers cool for 15 minutes. Sprinkle each with confectioners' sugar. Serve warm or at room temperature.

NUTRITION PER TURNOVER: calories: 283; protein: 3 g: fat: 16 g; carbohydrate: 33 g; fiber: 1 g; sodium: 179 mg; cholesterol: 25 mg

Cherry-Walnut Turnovers

Crisp phyllo pastry envelops a dried cherry and walnut filling drenched with spicy cherry syrup. To enjoy every last bite of the syrup, serve with a scoop of vanilla ice cream.

MAKES: 10 TURNOVERS

2 cups walnuts, toasted and chopped

1 cup dried cherries, chopped

1/2 cup Spiced Cherry Syrup (recipe follows)

2 tablespoons honey

1 teaspoon grated lemon zest

1/2 teaspoon salt

20 frozen phyllo sheets, thawed

1/2 cup (1 stick) unsalted butter, melted

1/2 cup confectioners' sugar

1. Combine the walnuts, dried cherries, syrup, honey, lemon zest, and salt in a medium bowl and set aside. Preheat the oven to 375°F. Line a baking sheet with parchment paper.

2. Lay the phyllo on a clean, flat surface and cover the stack with a damp dish towel. Place one sheet of phyllo on your work surface and brush it with melted butter. Sprinkle it with about 1 teaspoon confectioners' sugar, top it with another phyllo sheet, and again brush with butter and sprinkle with sugar.

3. Place about 1/4 cup cherry-walnut filling in the bottom center of the phyllo, about 1 inch from the edge. Fold each phyllo strip around the filling into a triangle shape as you would fold a flag.

4. Transfer the turnover to the prepared baking sheet and brush the surface with melted butter. Repeat the filling and folding process using the remaining ingredients. Bake the turnovers until they are golden brown and crisp—about 15 minutes. Transfer to a wire rack to cool completely. They will keep in an airtight container for up to 2 days.

★ ★ ★

Spiced Cherry Syrup

You'll have leftover syrup after you've made the Cherry-Walnut Turnovers, but you'll find many good uses for it. One example is the Cherry Cola Cocktail: Fill an 8-ounce glass with crushed ice, then add ½ cup cola, 1½ tablespoons cherry syrup, and 1 ounce rum (optional). Stir and serve.

3 cups (about 1 pound) sweet cherries, pitted and halved

¼ cup water

¼ cup sugar

1 tablespoon fresh lemon juice

4 sticks cinnamon

Peel of 1 lemon, white pith removed, cut into 1-inch pieces

1. In a medium-size saucepan over medium-high heat, combine the cherries, water, sugar, lemon juice, cinnamon sticks, and lemon peel; bring to a boil. Reduce the heat and simmer until the cherries soften—10 to 15 minutes.

2. Remove the cinnamon sticks and lemon zest and run the mixture through a food mill into a medium-size bowl. Strain through a fine sieve. Transfer the syrup to an airtight container and refrigerate for up to 3 days. Makes about 1 cup.

NUTRITION PER TURNOVER: calories: 565; protein: 9 g; fat: 31; carbohydrate: 67 g; fiber: 4 g; sodium: 412 mg; cholesterol: 31 mg

Fig and Brie Turnovers

These flaky phyllo-wrapped turnovers pair nicely with a crisp white wine. For a terrific variation, try adding blue cheese to the fig and caramelized onion filling instead of Brie.

MAKES: 10 TURNOVERS

- **1 tablespoon unsalted butter**

- **2 medium onions, chopped (about 2 cups)**

- **³/₄ cup apple cider**

- **1 tablespoon honey**

- **³/₄ cup dried figs, coarsely chopped**

- **8 frozen phyllo sheets, thawed**

- **¹/₄ teaspoon ground black pepper**

- **8 ounces Brie cheese, cut into pieces**

- **Olive oil cooking spray**

1. In a large nonstick skillet, melt the butter over medium heat. Add the onions and cook, stirring occasionally, until they are golden brown and caramelized—20 to 30 minutes. Set aside.

2. Meanwhile, hydrate the figs: In a small saucepan over medium-high heat, bring the cider and honey to a boil. Remove the pan from the heat, add the figs, and cover. Allow the figs to sit until softened—about 30 minutes. Drain and set aside. Preheat the oven to 375°F and position a rack in the top third.

3. Remove the phyllo from the package and cover it with a dampened dish towel. Place a sheet of phyllo on the work surface, spray it with cooking spray, and cover it with a sheet of plastic wrap, pressing to allow the spray to penetrate the dough. Remove the plastic wrap and layer on another sheet of phyllo. Repeat the procedure with the remaining sheets of phyllo. Sprinkle the top layer of dough evenly with pepper.

4. Cut the phyllo dough lengthwise into 5 equal strips, then cut each strip in half horizontally (this task is easiest with a pizza wheel). Place 1¹/₂ tablespoons cheese at the bottom of each strip, top it with 2 teaspoons figs and 1 tablespoon caramelized onion; fold each strip around the filling into a triangle shape as you would fold a flag.

5. Bake the turnovers for 20 minutes, or until the tops are lightly browned. Transfer to a wire rack to cool completely. Serve warm.

NUTRITION PER TURNOVER: calories: 207; protein: 7 g; fat: 9 g; carbohydrate: 26g; fiber: 2.5 g; sodium: 393 mg; cholesterol: 20 mg

Quiche Lorraine Empanadas

No utensils are needed to dig into this handheld version of quiche Lorraine. These are a cinch to make (you can whip them up even faster if you substitute store-bought pie dough). Serve them with a simple green salad for a lazy Sunday brunch.

MAKES: 6 EMPANADAS

2 cups all-purpose flour

³/₄ teaspoon salt

11 tablespoons unsalted butter

¹/₃ cup ice water

¹/₄ cup chopped yellow onion

3 large eggs

2 large egg yolks

¹/₂ cup plus 3 tablespoons heavy cream

¹/₄ teaspoon ground black pepper

¹/₄ teaspoon freshly grated nutmeg

1¹/₂ cups grated Gruyère cheese

6 slices thickly cut bacon, cooked and chopped

1. Pulse the flour, ¹/₂ teaspoon salt, and 10 tablespoons butter in the bowl of a food processor fitted with a metal blade until the mixture resembles coarse meal. Drizzle in the ice water in a steady stream just until a dough forms (you may not need to use it all). Turn the dough out of the bowl and pat it into a disk. Wrap it with plastic and chill for 1 hour.

2. Heat the remaining 1 tablespoon butter in a medium-size frying pan over medium heat. Add the onion and cook until soft, about 4 minutes. Reduce the heat to medium-low. In a medium-size bowl, whisk together the eggs, egg yolks, all but 1 tablespoon cream, remaining ¹/₄ teaspoon salt, pepper, and nutmeg. Add 1 cup Gruyère and pour the egg mixture into the pan with the onions. Whisk until the eggs just begin to set, 8 to 10 minutes. Transfer the mixture to a bowl and stir to cool. Add the bacon and set aside.

< 138 >

3. Preheat the oven to 425°F and line a baking pan with parchment paper. Divide the dough into 6 equal pieces and roll each into an 8-inch round. Divide the filling among the dough rounds and sprinkle the remaining ½ cup Gruyère over all. Fold the dough over and crimp the edges with the tines of a fork to seal. Transfer the empanadas to the prepared baking pan. Brush them with the remaining 1 tablespoon cream and bake until golden—about 20 minutes. Transfer to a wire rack to cool. Serve warm.

NUTRITION PER EMPANADA: calories: 765; protein: 22 g; fat: 60 g; carbohydrate: 34 g; fiber: 1.5 g; sodium: 753 mg; cholesterol: 319 mg

metric equivalents charts

The recipes in this book use the standard U.S. method for measuring liquid and dry or solid ingredients (teaspoons, tablespoons, and cups). The information on this chart is provided to help cooks outside the United States successfully use these recipes. All equivalents are approximate.

METRIC EQUIVALENTS
FOR DIFFERENT TYPES OF INGREDIENTS

A standard cup measure of a dry or solid ingredient will vary in weight depending on the type of ingredient. A standard cup of liquid is the same volume for any type of liquid. Use the following chart when converting standard cup measures to grams (weight) or milliliters (volume).

Standard Cup	Fine Powder (e.g., flour)	Grain (e.g., rice)	Liquid Granular (e.g., sugar)	Solids (e.g., butter)	Liquid (e.g., milk)
1	140 g	150 g	190 g	200 g	240 ml
3/4	105 g	113 g	143 g	150 g	180 ml
2/3	93 g	100 g	125 g	133 g	160 ml
1/2	70 g	75 g	95 g	100 g	120 ml
1/3	47 g	50 g	63 g	67 g	80 ml
1/4	35 g	38 g	48 g	50 g	60 ml
1/8	18 g	19 g	24 g	25 g	30 ml

USEFUL EQUIVALENTS FOR LIQUID INGREDIENTS BY VOLUME

1/4 tsp =				1 ml
1/2 tsp =				2 ml
1 tsp =				5 ml
3 tsp =	1 tblsp =		1/2 fl oz =	15 ml
	2 tblsp =	1/8 cup =	1 fl oz =	30 ml
	4 tblsp =	1/4 cup =	2 fl oz =	60 ml
	5 1/3 tblsp =	1/3 cup =	3 fl oz =	80 ml
	8 tblsp =	1/2 cup =	4 fl oz =	120 ml
	10 2/3 tblsp =	2/3 cup =	5 fl oz =	160 ml
	12 tblsp =	3/4 cup =	6 fl oz =	180 ml
	16 tblsp =	1 cup =	8 fl oz =	240 ml
	1 pt =	2 cups =	16 fl oz =	480 ml
	1 qt =	4 cups =	32 fl oz =	960 ml
			33 fl oz =	1000 ml = 1 L

USEFUL EQUIVALENTS FOR LENGTH

(To convert inches to centimeters, multiply the number of inches by 2.5.)

1 in =			2.5 cm =	
6 in =	1/2 ft =		15 cm =	
12 in =	1 ft =		30 cm =	
36 in =	3 ft =	1 yd =	90 cm =	
40 in =			100 cm =	1 m

USEFUL EQUIVALENTS FOR DRY INGREDIENTS BY WEIGHT

(To convert ounces to grams, multiply the number of ounces by 30.)

1 oz =	1/16 lb =	30 g
4 oz =	1/4 lb =	120 g
8 oz =	1/2 lb =	240 g
12 oz =	3/4 lb =	360 g
16 oz =	1 lb =	480 g

USEFUL EQUIVALENTS FOR COOKING/OVEN TEMPERATURES

	Farenheit	Celcius	Gas Mark
Freeze Water	32° F	0° C	
Room Temp.	68° F	20° C	
Boil Water	212° F	100° C	
Bake	325° F	160° C	3
	350° F	180° C	4
	375° F	190° C	5
	400° F	200° C	6
	425° F	220° C	7
	450° F	230° C	8

index

photography credits

Front Cover: Ellen Silverman
Miki Duisterhof: 113
Dasha Wright Ewing: 44
Foodpix: Alison Miksch: 117
Dana Gallagher: 6
Thayer Allison Gowdy: 1, 10, 12, 16, 60, 68, 84, 87, 97, 101
Getty Images: Judd Pilossof: 2
John Granen: 15, 131
Gridley and Graves: 9
iStockphoto: 30, 45, 46, 53; Marie Fields: 66; Scott Griessel: 123; Michal Karbowiak: 45;
Robert Linton: 58
Ray Kachatorian: 128
Keller & Keller: 105
Kate Mathis: 139
Andrew McCaul: 134
Alison Miksch: 126, 132
Steven Mark Needham: 17, 18, 19 (pie crusts), 56, 57, 82, 83
Janis Nicoly: 99
Marcus Nilsson: 71, 72, 102, 110, 115
Helen Norman: 19 (child), 89, 94, 136, 140
Steven Randazzo: 11, 22, 34, 65, 91
Alan Richardson: 20, 80
Cole Riggs: 106
Tina Rupp: 26
Charles Schiller: 29, 49, 51, 120, 130
Gitte Staerbo: 32
Ann Stratton: 54, 63, 103, 119
Ellen Silverman: 38, 47, 77, 93
Dasha Wright: 8

special thanks

Our thanks to the following for contributing recipes to this book.

Bird-in-Hand Bakery: 72
Crown Restaurant: 70
The Farm Chicks: 59, 60, 68, 85, 86, 96, 100
Golden Lamb: 103
Louie's Backyard: 114
Sweet Surrender Dessert Café: 110

Recipe for

From the kitchen of

Recipe for _____

From the kitchen of _____

Recipe for

From the kitchen of

Recipe for

From the kitchen of

Recipe for

From the kitchen of

Recipe for _____

From the kitchen of _____

Recipe for

From the kitchen of

Recipe for

From the kitchen of